Classical Latin, Crea

Latin *for* Children

ACTIVITY BOOK!

Primer A

Rob Baddorf with
Dr. Christopher Perrin

Latin for Children Primer A • Activity Book

Classical Academic Press
515 S. 32nd Street
Camp Hill, PA 17011

www.ClassicalAcademicPress.com

ISBN: 978-1-60051-005-2

Puzzles designed & illustrated by:
Rob Baddorf

KP.02.24

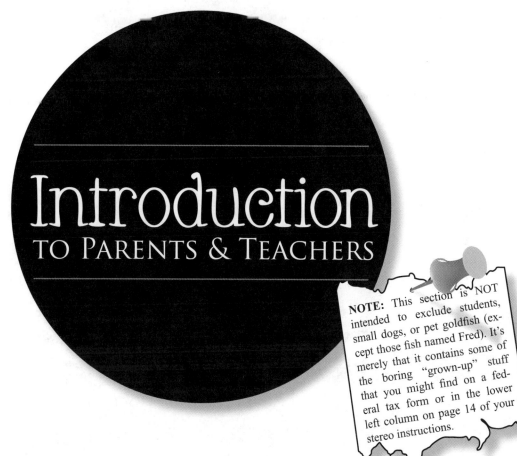

Introduction
TO PARENTS & TEACHERS

NOTE: This section is NOT intended to exclude students, small dogs, or pet goldfish (except those fish named Fred). It's merely that it contains some of the boring "grown-up" stuff that you might find on a federal tax form or in the lower left column on page 14 of your stereo instructions.

This book is intended as a learning aid for students studying Latin with the *Latin for Children Primer A* textbook. It follows that textbook chapter for chapter. Thus, the words learned in chapter 3 of the textbook correlate to those in chapter 3 of this activity book (but, as review, activities might also contain words and concepts learned from previous chapters).

Not all puzzles will appeal to all students. Feel free to have students do all the puzzles, attempt a challenging puzzle only to return to it later, or, with your permission, skip some entirely. Our goal is not to stump the students with impossible puzzles but rather, with a reasonable sense of challenge, have students continue practicing their Latin in a setting of fun, games, and playfulness.

NOTE:
Unless otherwise specified, all nouns featured in the puzzles will be singular and nominative (the first form listed in the LFC Primer vocabulary lists). Unless otherwise specified, adjectives featured in these puzzles will be masculine, singular, nominative (the first form listed in the LFC Primer vocabulary lists).

A few ideas . . .

• Have students use highlighters for the word search puzzles. This will help minimize the muddle of circles.

• Have students use colored pencils on the matching games to delineate one line from another.

• Encourage students to work together (when possible) on some of the more challenging puzzles.

• Have students create their own puzzles and games.

Don't forget, on page 147:

Latin on the High Seas!

GROUP GAME
BASED ON *LATIN FOR CHILDREN PRIMER A*

Chapter One

Word Crossing

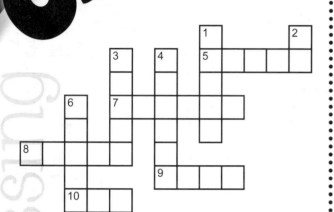

Across
5. I tell
7. I work
8. gate
9. water
10. I love

Down
1. I enter
2. I give
3. forest
4. story
6. earth

Oops!

We lost the answers to the crossword puzzle somewhere in this mess. Help us find 'em and then fill in the crossword (or vice versa if you're really clever!).

```
T M K B X L J Y L U S
B E W M D T H P Y V R
V Q R A L R U O R N M
I J L R V J Q R C B K
F I O K A Y B T V Q Q
I N T R Ō A D A E D Y
G B M G L Q E Ō M N C
U M N B U U C K O C Z
S B E Z W A R H X N N
A U I N G Z E S P O R
L A M Ō F J G F G R E
I A B Q G F C M X B P
L R B A L I F A V N D
W L S Ō J L Z L B W L
N H E X R U S I L V A
L A B M Y Ō A L H A Q
C K R G K W D A H Z Z
N B Q R W K G R C S I
N U K S Ō C X R I A X
Z G F D N O T I O S P
```

BONUS: Can you find the one missing chapter vocabulary word that's not listed in the word search? What is it? _____

"I Love"	SINGULAR	PLURAL
____ person		
2nd p___son		
3____ per____		

ENTER THE MAZE . . .

There are <u>three</u> Latin words stuck in the maze. You need to go in there (if you dare) and find exactly which three words are on the pathway to the exit. Find those words and only those words, then enter them in the space provided at the bottom of the page. You might want to use a pencil until you find the correct path . . .

The three Latin words are: _____, _____, _____

Can you translate them? _____, _____, _____

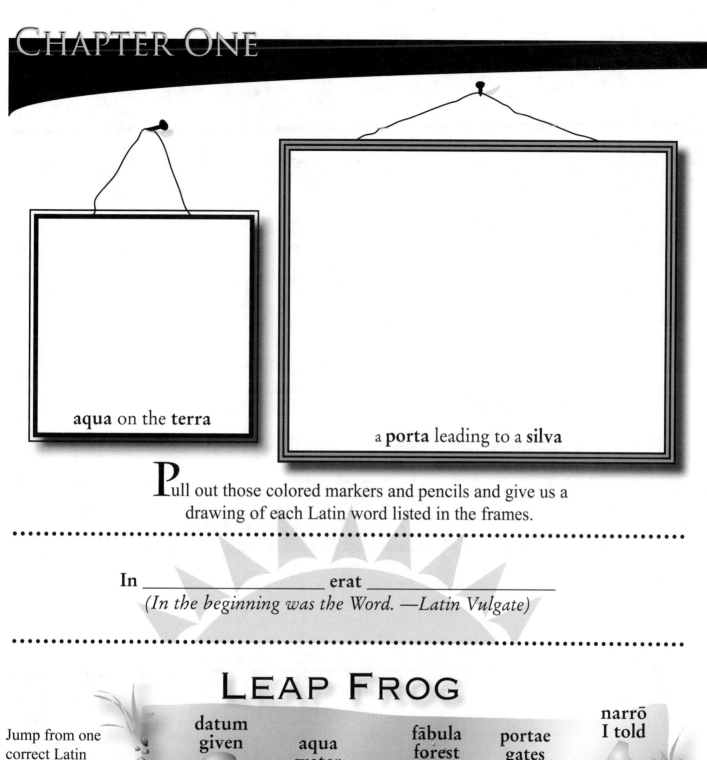

aqua on the **terra**

a **porta** leading to a **silva**

Pull out those colored markers and pencils and give us a
drawing of each Latin word listed in the frames.

· ·

In _____ **erat** _____

(In the beginning was the Word. —Latin Vulgate)

· ·

LEAP FROG

Jump from one
correct Latin
rock to another.
Draw a line to
connect them.

Make sure
to avoid the
incorrect Latin
rocks or you'll
slip into the
muddy water!

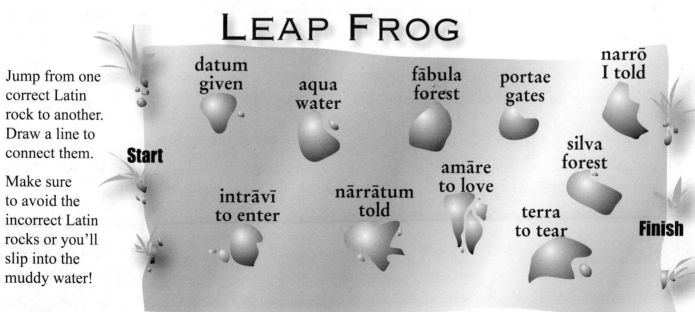

datum
given

aqua
water

fābula
forest

portae
gates

narrō
I told

Start

silva
forest

intrāvī
to enter

nārrātum
told

amāre
to love

terra
to tear

Finish

Chapter Two

MIX & MATCH

Can you draw a line between the correct person/number and its appropriate pronoun(s)?

It

I

We

You

He

You (all)

She

They

3rd-Person Plural

1st-Person Singular

2nd-Person Plural

1st-Person Plural

2nd-Person Singular

3rd-Person Singular

Across
3. page
5. fatherland
8. table
9. island

Down
1. dinner
2. ditch
4. breeze
6. queen
7. road, way
8. turning point, goal

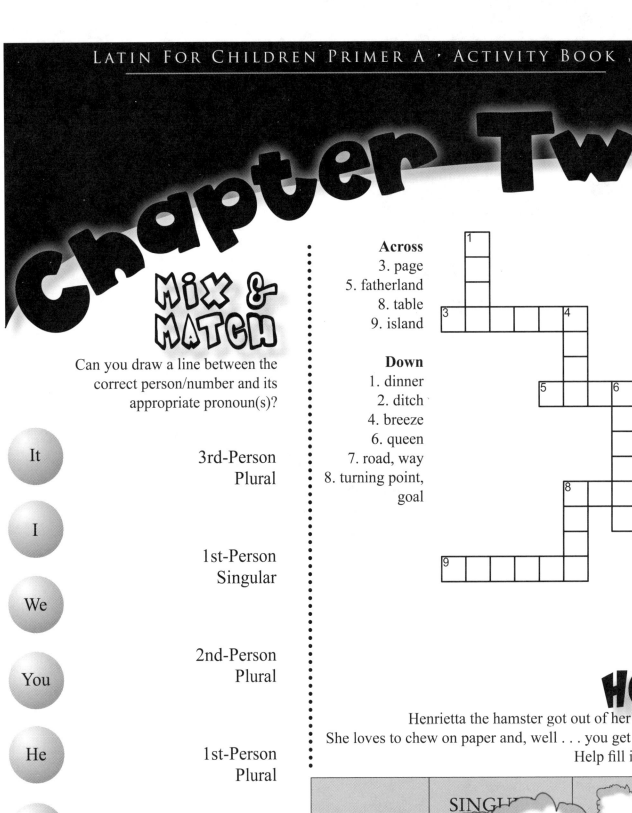

HOLES

Henrietta the hamster got out of her cage again. She loves to chew on paper and, well . . . you get the picture. Help fill in the holes.

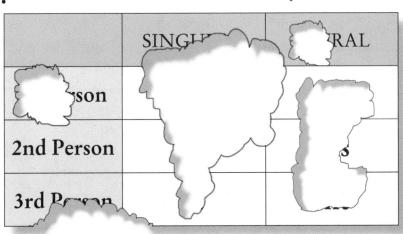

	SINGULAR	PLURAL
1st Person		
2nd Person		
3rd Person		

DOUBLE DUTY

OK, you enter the damp, dark maze looking for <u>three</u> correct <u>English</u> words this time. When you find them, write them under their maze and translate them into Latin. Then you can enter the second maze and look for the <u>three</u> correct <u>Latin</u> words. Translate them into English at the bottom of the page . . . if you can find them!

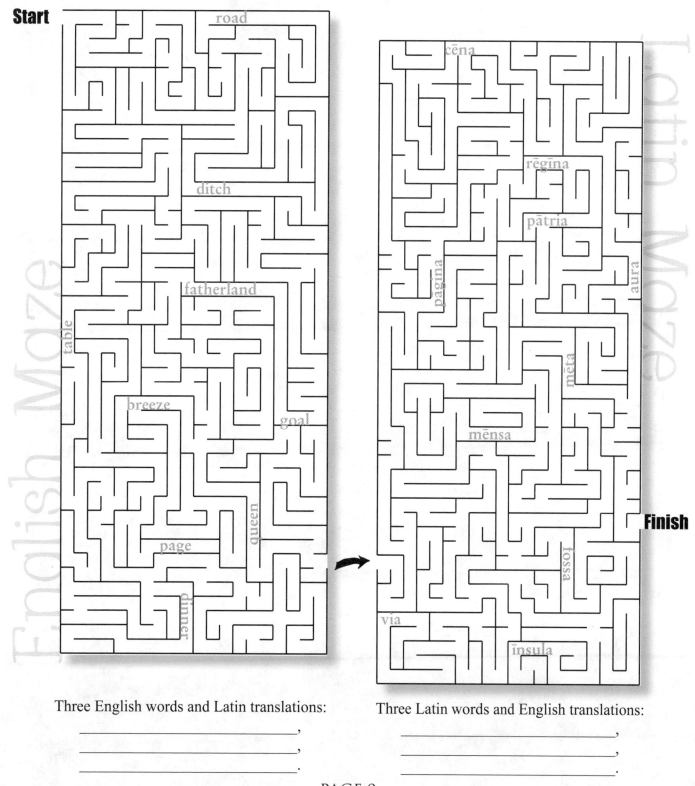

Three English words and Latin translations:

_____,

_____,

_____.

Three Latin words and English translations:

_____,

_____,

_____.

TREASURE MAP

Something that looks like a treasure map washed ashore, matie. Solve each puzzle (fill in the blanks), then move on toward the treasure!

Chapter Three

GIRLY NOUNS

Sister Susie wants to have a tea party, but she's not sure which tea bags go with which cups. Can you help by drawing a line from the tea bags to the correct teacups? Make sure to match <u>both words</u> on each item.

īra
via

cēna
aura

cēna
unda

īnsula
fenestra

pāgina
aura

Sugar

īnsula
esse

unda
glōria

rēgina
sum

sum
via

dinner	island	queen	I am	anger	dinner	page	wave	island
breeze	window	I am	road	road	wave	breeze	glory	to be

∙∙∙

_____ virumque _____

(Of arms _____ *I sing. —Vergil's* _____ *)*

CHAPTER THREE

Here's a chance to do what you've always
dreamed of—clean up the table!
Fill in the blanks and we'll consider letting
someone else do the dishes!
Use your textbook if you need help.

Case	Noun Job	Singular	Plural
	SN, PrN		**mēnsae:** tables
Genitive			
		mēnsae:	
Accusative			**mēnsās:** the tables
	OP		

What does it mean?

Do you remember from your
English lessons what these
abbreviations mean?

SN _____

PrN _____

PNA _____

IO _____

DO _____

OP_____

PAGE 12

Word Crossing

Across
1. I stand
4. ditch
5. glory
7. wave
9. I am
10. anger
13. fatherland
14. breeze
15. I prepare
17. story

Down
1. I look at
2. road, way
3. queen
4. window
6. island
8. maidservant
11. I wander
12. gate
16. water

Review

Redraw the upper tiles to fit in the blank spaces below to find the hidden phrase. The first block is redrawn for you. How soon can you guess the phrase?

b u	t f	e o	r w	~~L a t~~	i s
d i n	g s ,	a n y	i n	e w e	s .
e n	a l	o r d	a n g	f m	u a g

L a t					

Chapter Four

What a mess!

Somewhere in there are all of this week's vocabulary words. If you look hard enough, you will find a few review words as well. Can you find them all?

Find:

girl ☐
woman ☐
daughter ☐
sister ☐
female teacher ☐
female student ☐
female master ☐
female servant ☐
female slave ☐
female friend ☐

```
D M T S I E F X S I L N
S I V Q C I Ē F Y B B Ā
Q G S L F L M X F S S R
C C H C S H I M L N I R
Y I F N I C N V A N L Ō
Z I P H K P A L F F V C
V Z U I W Z U A H Ī J P
C Q S W O M T L H L S Z
P Q D O M I N A A I T I
I U N D X U T R K A Ō Y
T M E Y K C L L R R F U
X F Ē L E R R Ō H K F A
P S A N L J F G W Q J Q
G O N M S A S E R V A U
Z V A W U A Y H B W W A
S F K Q M L A T K I V R
N I R T A P A M S V G T
I E Y X G R A C Ī U V Q
J T X U I V O R Y C Q Q
G W D O S T Z J Ō T A V
A R U E T A W S U Z U S
R Z B O R S M Y S S Z Y
P A T Y A V W Z H C M A
O C E D A R R B B I W K
N Q P L Q Z P Q T A W Z
L W V T K M L R P H I K
L X K V Q G O S A B T X
Q C E E F H Y A T T P D
G E R M Ā N A F O S S A
K A J L R Q I J U B Y C
```

Start

Finish

MAZE PHAZE

Traverse the maze and record the numbers, in order, that you cross. Then, using the code block to the right, find the secret Latin word.

Code Letters						
F						
6						
Maze Numbers						

1	2	3	4	5	6	7	8	9	10	11	12	13
A	B	C	D	E	F	G	H	I	J	K	L	M

14	15	16	17	18	19	20	21	22	23	24	25	26
N	O	P	Q	R	S	T	U	V	W	X	Y	Z

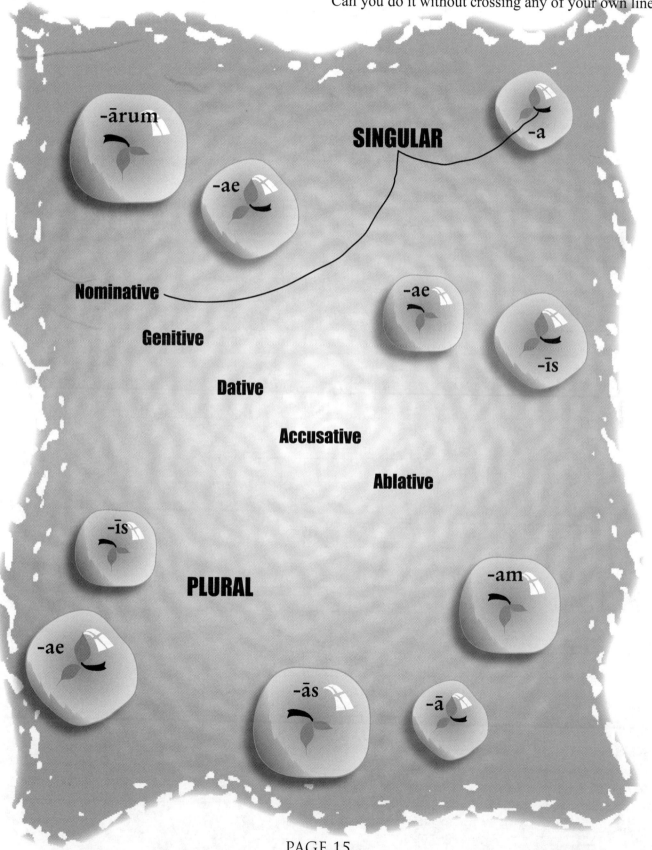

CHAPTER FOUR

Bobbing for Davus

Connect the apples with a line to the correct <u>case</u> and then the correct <u>number</u>.
Can you do it without crossing any of your own lines?

-ārum

-ae

SINGULAR

-a

Nominative

-ae

Genitive

-īs

Dative

Accusative

Ablative

-īs

PLURAL

-am

-ae

-ās

-ā

SCRAMBLE BRAMBLE

Can you unscramble these words and find this week's vocabulary within them?
Once unscrambled, use the letters that have numbers underneath to find the mystery phrase.

LUEPAL, GLRI

P U E L L A , G I R L
 10

MDNIAO, AMFELE MESATR

[ ][ ][ ][ ][ ][ ] , [ ][ ][ ][ ][ ][ ] [ ][ ][ ][ ][ ][ ]
                                          2   13

AISTMGAR, AFEEML HCTAERE

[ ][ ][ ][ ][ ][ ][ ][ ] , [ ][ ][ ][ ][ ][ ] [ ][ ][ ][ ][ ][ ][ ]
              1

MĀNARGE, ITRSES

[ ][ ][ ][ ][ ][ ][ ] , [ ][ ][ ][ ][ ][ ]
                                    4

LCPIUSIAD, EALFEM TDTSEUN

[ ][ ][ ][ ][ ][ ][ ][ ][ ] , [ ][ ][ ][ ][ ][ ] [ ][ ][ ][ ][ ][ ][ ]
            5   12   15

LAMUFA, FMEALE ENTVASR

[ ][ ][ ][ ][ ][ ] , [ ][ ][ ][ ][ ][ ] [ ][ ][ ][ ][ ][ ][ ][ ]
                                              6   9

AREVS, EAEFML ELVAS

[ ][ ][ ][ ][ ] , [ ][ ][ ][ ][ ][ ] [ ][ ][ ][ ][ ]
                            11

IĒFANM, NAWMO

[ ][ ][ ][ ][ ][ ] , [ ][ ][ ][ ][ ]
                             7

ĪMACA, EAMLEF DEFINR

[ ][ ][ ][ ][ ] , [ ][ ][ ][ ][ ][ ] [ ][ ][ ][ ][ ][ ]
   14   3

FIALĪ, DUEAHTGR

[ ][ ][ ][ ][ ][ ] , [ ][ ][ ][ ][ ][ ][ ][ ]
        8

[ ] ' [ ] [ ][ ][ ][ ][ ][ ][ ] G [ ][ ][ ][ ][ ] !
1   2   3 4 5 6 7 8 9 10   11 12 13 14 15

MYSTERY PHRASE

REVIEW

Chapter Five

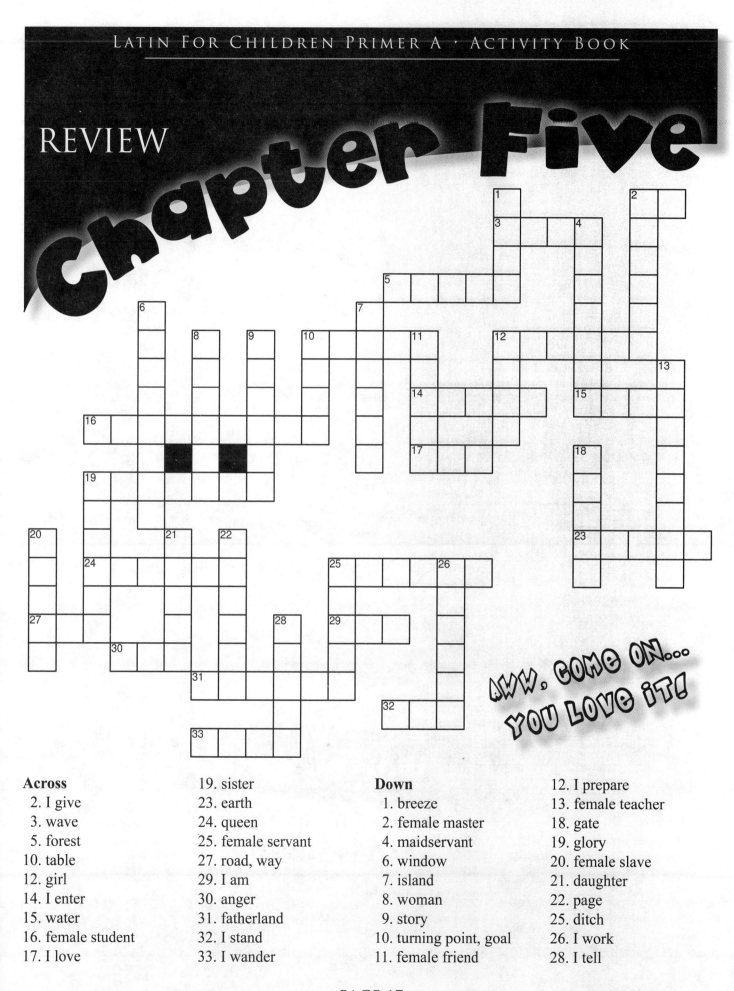

AWW, COME ON... YOU LOVE IT!

Across

2. I give
3. wave
5. forest
10. table
12. girl
14. I enter
15. water
16. female student
17. I love
19. sister
23. earth
24. queen
25. female servant
27. road, way
29. I am
30. anger
31. fatherland
32. I stand
33. I wander

Down

1. breeze
2. female master
4. maidservant
6. window
7. island
8. woman
9. story
10. turning point, goal
11. female friend
12. I prepare
13. female teacher
18. gate
19. glory
20. female slave
21. daughter
22. page
25. ditch
26. I work
28. I tell

Scan the articles below and circle any words that you recognize as derivatives from Latin words you've learned so far. Do your best.

Derivative Newspaper

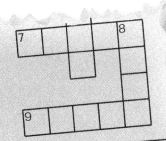

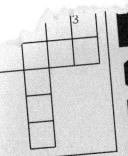

ated that an error as occured in the blishing of the article. The family of blue aquatic dolphins was not what as giving off a wonderful aroma on the BBQ it was the he tuna steaks that sent off the smell. ∎

___

he only portable sh in the tank. You move it upstairs it won't help the old problem. t it free, fabulous d all in one easy yment. No money wn. We're here to our best & serve the only way t we know. Yes, rambling on and but I've got to me up with more l more text just to the sp More-there a re us fill in

Need a Plumber?

Are your pipes getting old? Are they turning into fossils? Let REGAL PIPE SERVICE come and look things over. We're professional, amicable, and we all wear belts. Don't let freestanding, static water build up in your sink. We can roto route almost any problem—big or small.

Is your hot water not staying hot? We can put insulation on all your pipes to give you the most energy-efficient plumbing possible.

Call us now! 555-3244

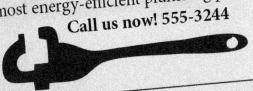

The Way to SAVINGS

Don't be a spectator anymore! Go to your nearest mall and BUY, BUY, BUY! You'll love all that junk for

CUTES BABY AWAR

This year's a winner was an pick. The female picked a family such a cute chil thought it migl crime.

Not to domin competition a child, who w cute as well, w brought into ning.

Irritating the sk fair amount of powder was throughout the c tition a

Derivative Roundup

Draw a line to match the English derivative to its Latin origin.

donation	fēmina
magistrate	magistra
page	pātria
patriotic	dō
ancillary	domina
serve	nārrō
dominate	terra
fable	ancilla
insular	pāgina
aroma	amō
fossil	spectō
feminine	serva
extraterrestrial	fābula
aquatic	īnsula
spectacle	aqua
amorous	aura
narration	fossa

Climb the Tree

Can you start at the bottom and climb your way to the top, filling in the blanks as you go?

_____ I stand

spectō _____

sum _____

fēmina _____

_____ sister

magistra _____

discipula _____

domina _____

intrō _____

labōrō _____

_____ story

fossa _____

fīlia _____

narrō _____

_____ way

aqua _____

porta _____

_____ forest

puella _____

_____ earth

parō _____

mēnsa _____

mēta _____

_____ page

cēna _____

Chapter Six

Word Crossing

Across

6. queen
10. I work
11. student (female)
14. son
15. story
16. friend (male)
17. student/disciple (male)
19. man

Down

1. teacher/master (male)
2. water
3. slave (male)
4. gate
5. master (female)
7. brother
8. servant (male)
9. I tell
12. anger
13. breeze
17. master (male)
18. boy

Smokin'

Put out the fire by re-creating (redrawing) the chart!

Case		Singular		Plural
Nominative	SN,	ludus- "school"		dī- "schools"
Genitive	PNA	dī - "of the school"		n- "of the sc..."
Dative	IO	..dō- "to/for the s..		for the schools"
Accus...	O, OP	ludum- "the..		
Al...	..OP			..chools"

Gotta Go!

Can you help direct these Latin words toward the correct doorway? Draw a line from the Latin words to the symbols (gender) on the doors. Then write the translation underneath each word.

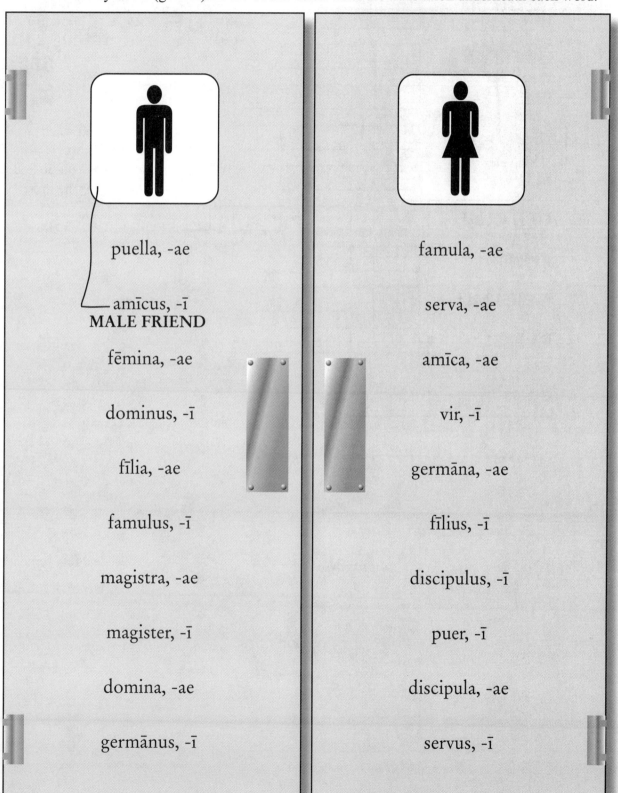

puella, -ae

amīcus, -ī
MALE FRIEND

fēmina, -ae

dominus, -ī

fīlia, -ae

famulus, -ī

magistra, -ae

magister, -ī

domina, -ae

germānus, -ī

famula, -ae

serva, -ae

amīca, -ae

vir, -ī

germāna, -ae

fīlius, -ī

discipulus, -ī

puer, -ī

discipula, -ae

servus, -ī

CHAPTER SIX

UN-SCRAMBLED EGGS

UDONSMI ☐☐☐☐☐☐☐
  4 5

IRV ☐☐☐

UACSĪM ☐☐☐☐☐

EMSAIRTG ☐☐☐☐☐☐☐
              7

UMGSEĀRN G☐☐☐☐☐☐
              6

SLĪFUI ☐☐☐☐☐
       2

UPILCUSDSI D☐☐☐☐☐☐☐☐☐
                   3

EPUR ☐☐☐☐

LASUFMU F☐☐☐☐☐☐

RVSESU ☐☐☐☐☐☐
       1

Unscramble each word to form one of this week's Latin words. Then use the numbered letters to discover the mystery phrase.

W☐☐☐ ☐☐☐☐!
 1 2 3 4 5 6 7

....

Cum _____, _____.
(When they are silent, they shout. —Cicero)

Write something about your **magistra** (if you have one).

Write a few sentences about your **magister** (if you have one).

PAGE 22

Chapter Seven

WHOA NELLIE!

Did we bite off more than we can chew? In this puzzle you will find only this week's vocabulary.

TRANSLATE . . . then find:

I watch (or guard) _____

to watch _____

I watched _____

watched _____

I shout _____

to shout _____

I shouted _____

shouted _____

I delay _____

to delay _____

I delayed _____

delayed _____

I live _____

to live _____

I lived _____

lived _____

I point out _____

to point out _____

I pointed out _____

pointed out _____

school, game _____

garden _____

wolf _____

ally, associate _____

water-carrier _____

```
D Z C X B W Y X P B L V N L M
D Ē M Ō N S T R Ā R E I O O S
V Ē M V I G I L Ā V Ī G Y O P
I C M Ō V G X V L N E I C A O
G H L Ō N Q L V C F Q L T Q E
I A Q Ā N S H A B I T Ā T U M
L B J L M S T J K C J T R Ā T
Ā I S D Z Ā T R V D H U J R A
R T E X T S T R Ā S H M G I R
E Ō W L K S O U Ō V O G L U D
C L Ā M Ā R E C M G Ī W T S Ā
C G O A H R I R I Q Y Y Z R T
M U H M Z Q W S D U R Q S P U
W S W K V V U C Ē V S A B C M
H A B I T Ā R E M V M E K Q I
T A R D Ā V Ī L Ō N I W Y R A
H O R T U S C U N F Z G Q A Q
K N O W M H L P S J D T I O O
U M O G Y Q Ā U T M R L Z L A
L C M J A A M S R A A M M D Ō
J Q U H C C Ō D Ā L F T D C R
H M P V C L P I T V S A W F E
B A B E V R Ā W U H O R U T X
X J B J L M L M M E P D D L H
L D G I X U S Ū Ā S C Ā R A H
E M V M T B T O D V S R Z A T
T A R D Ō Ā K N Y U Ī E M Z R
H Q Q P G B V U A G S I N P P
H V L X Z B Z Ī B O L R Q D E
H K D P G G T O F E V E B Q S
```

CHAPTER SEVEN

OK, this one is a little icy in spots, but don't let that keep you off the slopes. It's just that you'll be winding your way down the mountain a bit. Can you escape from the top of the mountain, translating as you go?

Ski Slopes

water-carrier

game

I shout

lived

pointed out

watched

Start

school

wolf

Finish

Six words found
(and translated):

ally

to live

_____

I watched

_____

_____

shouted

_____

to point out

_____

garden

_____

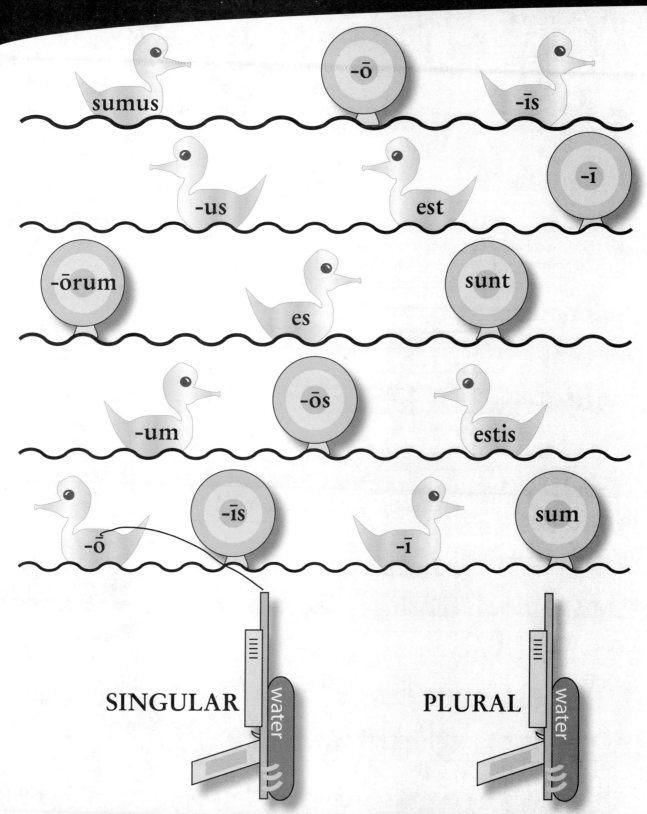

Use the water guns at the bottom to connect (draw a line) the correct singular and plural second-declension noun endings. Can you do **sum** (I am) as well?

CARNIVAL SHOOT-OUT!

Chapter Eight

BUMBLE JUMBLE

Each vocabulary word from this week got jumbled up. Can you straighten them out and find the hidden Latin phrase?

Need a **clue**? Look below.

1. ŌDUNM [ ][ ][ ][ ][ ]
   1

2. NOGPUŌP [ ][ ][ ][ ][ ][ ][ ]
   8

3. IXMILUAU [ ][ ][ ][ ][ ][ ][ ][ ]
   2

4. DANŌM [ ][ ][ ][ ][ ]
   4

5. ŌALBUM [ ][ ][ ][ ][ ][ ]
   10

6. IIEUIDFAMC [ ][ ][ ][ ][ ][ ][ ][ ][ ][ ]
   3

7. ULMACE [ ][ ][ ][ ][ ][ ]
   5

8. PGUNŌ [ ][ ][ ][ ][ ]
   9

9. EPUEMLXM [ ][ ][ ][ ][ ][ ][ ][ ]
   6

10. ŌNEC [ ][ ][ ][ ]
    7

[ ][ ][V][ ][ ] [ ][T][ ][R][ ][ ][ ][ ]
1 2 3 4 5   6   7 8 9 10

clues!

1. gift
2. I attack
3. help
4. I entrust
5. I walk
6. building
7. sky
8. I fight
9. example
10. I kill

ACME MEASURING STICK

Neuter Rule

For all neuter nouns, the

_____

and

_____

case forms are exactly the same.

Begin listing all the exceptions to the neuter rule:

_____

_____

dōnō: _____

Singular

dōnīs: _____

dōnī: _____

: by/with/from the gifts

	Nominative	
	Ablative	

: the gifts

Genitive

Plural

Accusative

_____ : the gift

: of the gifts

: gift

dōna: _____

: to/for the gift

Dative

Little Billy got a little excited about his birthday gift and opened it too fast. Now it's everywhere. Can you help him put the Latin table back together, filling in the blanks as needed? (See how Genitive has been placed underneath the Nominative box.) Draw arrows to place all of the contents in their proper box.

PARTY POOPER

Word Crossing

MISSING!

The crossword clues—what . . . what happened to them?!
Somehow all the Across and Down clues got stolen. They are scattered throughout the **next chapter** in this book. Can you find them and finish the puzzle?

Police Line — Do NOT Cross

It will take a sharp detective to find them all!

Example: Look on the far upper left-hand corner of page 29.

Chapter nine

Word Hunt

You know the drill by now. Find all of this week's words—and if you happen to stumble across a few review vocabulary words, circle them as well. Translate them below.

Down: 10. I entrusted 12. example

Across: 11. to entrust 16. I killed

```
F D T U B N N V G G L H H U F E H X H L F V T I F M T M P E
L R G M E P A C R I A H G I O E V P O X Ū R L Q K A X B R C
C S C U N W B N O V V U O M R U E R N L U D Ū K W N T A A S
C M F P E R Ī C U L U M D H U I N Z G P F R U M F D X U E Z
S K S R F R P B F Q H T G I M M D D T E R R A S E Ō A D M Y
T K I J I P W B B F G X A Y U N T D A B U C X W L N J V I G
E P V F C Q L F Q V V C S L J M U J R O U X X O S L T L U Z
W D F B I M X I B W S E T Y H O J D K L R W R M B J M U M Q
I P W I U O P P I D U M R C O L L U M S E E O W L K B C M X
C Y R U M O H T D X K F U R X W U K Q D R D T H B L N D H T
S I W W E Y B I C J K P M G C Z C O C G M Z L U L N W W O O
X J I O E C T R V E C Ē N A T C H T I D L W J W S W J D P R
```

Find above, then translate:

fātum _____

forum _____

oppidum _____

perīculum _____

frūmentum _____

praemium _____

astrum _____

beneficium _____

gaudium _____

collum _____

EXTRA WORDS FOUND:

Job Board

In Latin, you can usually tell what the subject of a sentence is because it is in the _____ case.

Another Maze, Ugh!

For those of you who don't like mazes all that much, this one's for you!

Start   **Finish**

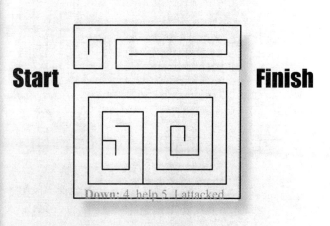

Down: 4. help 5. I attacked

Down: 1. killed 2. walked 6. I fight 7. to attack

Another Maze, Wee–whooo!

For those of you who <u>do</u> like a good ole Latin maze, here's a doozy!
When it comes to going under the bridge, follow your path straight (use
the gray arrow). For those who <u>don't</u> like mazes, cross the bridge,
translating as you go, then head on to the next page!

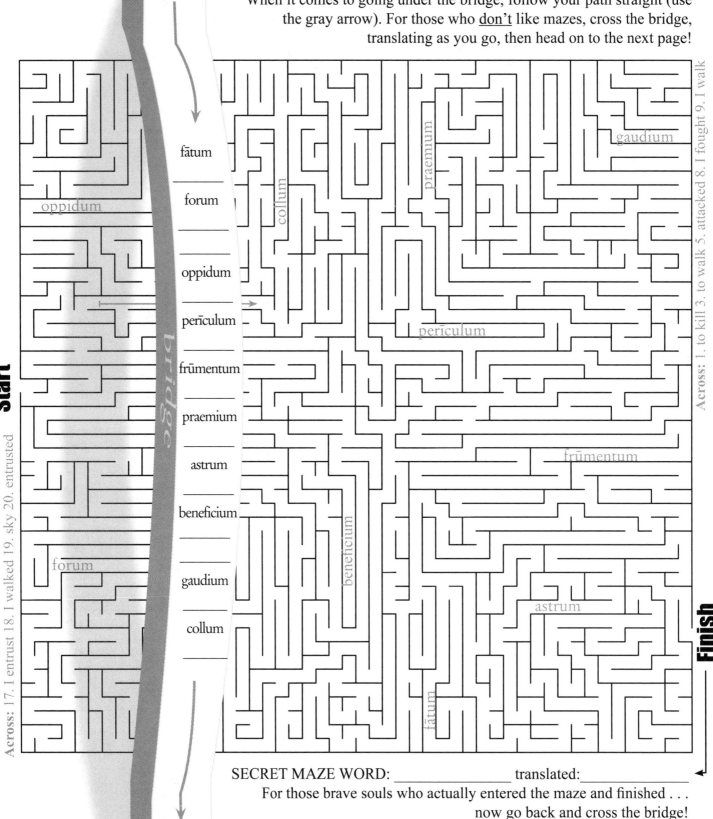

Start

Across: 17. I entrust 18. I walked 19. sky 20. entrusted

Across: 1. to kill 3. to walk 5. attacked 8. I fought 9. I walk

Finish

bridge

fātum
_____
forum
_____
oppidum
_____
perīculum
_____
frūmentum
_____
praemium
_____
astrum
_____
beneficium
_____
gaudium
_____
collum
_____

next
page

SECRET MAZE WORD: _____ translated: _____
For those brave souls who actually entered the maze and finished . . .
now go back and cross the bridge!

CHAPTER NINE

2ND DNNE

Second-declension neuter noun endings—that wasn't obvious?
It's time—pardon the pun—to connect the noun endings to their correct role in the sentence.
From the top down, can you draw a line connecting them correctly?

Down: 9. building 13. I kill 14. gift 15. fought

-um -īs -ō -a -um -ō -ī -a -ōrum -īs

(SN) (PN) (PNA) (IO) (DO) (OP)

subject

possessive noun

predicate nominative

object of the preposition

indirect object

direct object

REVIEW

Chapter 10

Doesn't look that big, huh?!
Then maybe you need to
turn and look at the next
three pages!

Use the Across and Down
clues on the next two pages
to fill in this behemoth
puzzle.

NOTE: The puzzle does
overlap from one page to the
next.

Attack of the Monstrous Crossword!

CHAPTER 10

monster
drool

ACROSS

6. neck
9. I attack
10. I give
11. page
13. I shout
14. earth
16. town
18. anger
20. window
21. I fight
23. example
30. slave (female)
32. dinner

33. I kill
34. garden
35. water-carrier
36. slave (male)
37. student/disciple
    (male)
39. I stand
40. building
45. I love
47. help
48. I enter
50. breeze
52. servant (male)
53. I entrust

54. girl
55. ally
57. friend (male)
60. teacher (female)
61. queen
65. road, way
66. maidservant
68. grain
70. gift
71. water
72. I watch (or guard)
73. wolf

CHAPTER 10

DOWN
1. benefit, gift
2. public square
3. friend (female)
4. ditch
5. I am
7. master (male)
8. I look at
10. female master
11. reward
12. son

13. sky
15. I wander
17. boy
19. star
20. fate
22. glory
24. I prepare
25. wave
26. woman
27. brother
28. student (female)
29. I delay
31. school, game
34. I live
38. I point out
41. story
42. turning point, goal
43. sister
44. man
46. teacher/master (male)
49. gate
51. I work
53. table
54. fatherland
56. forest
58. island

59. servant (female)
62. joy
63. I walk
64. danger
67. I tell
69. daughter

KEEP OUT!

Aww, that wasn't so scary, now was it?

Chapter 11

EXPLŌRĀRE

_____ cōgitō
_____ dubitō
_____ magnus
_____ dubitāvī
_____ parvum
_____ vērus
_____ falsa
_____ cōgitāre
_____ mūtāre

Fill in the space as you mine for lost diamonds.
Translate them all and find the mother lode!

parvus _____
mūtāvī _____
creāvī _____
vērum _____

explōrō _____
creō _____
mūtātum _____
dubitāre _____
magnum _____
creātum _____
mūtō _____
falsum _____

cōgitātum _____
dubitātum _____
dubius _____

_____
ergo _____.

"I _____
therefore I
_____."
—Descartes

_____ large, great
_____ to change
_____ changed
_____ false
_____ small
_____ large, great
_____ small
_____ false
_____ true

I doubt _____
small _____
true _____
I think _____
true _____
false _____
doubtful _____
I change _____
I explore _____
created _____
I create _____
I doubted _____
to doubt _____

WHAT'S FOR DINNER?

With what is being offered on the menu, can you correctly match all of the correct side dishes to create a fabulous Latin meal? Circle the correct choices.

Menu: Adjective Endings

-us

	Singular		Plural		
CASE	Nom.	Gen.	Dat.	Acc.	Abl.
Masculine		Feminine		Neuter	

-ō

Singular		
Plural		
CASE	Nom.	Gen.
(Dat.)	Acc.	Abl.
Masculine		
Feminine		
(Neuter)		

-ārum

	Singular		Plural		
CASE	Nom.	Gen.	Dat.	Acc.	Abl.
Masculine		Feminine		Neuter	

-īs

Singular		
Plural		
CASE	Nom.	Gen.
(Dat.)	Acc.	Abl.
Masculine		
(Feminine)		
Neuter		

-ōs

	Singular		Plural		
CASE	Nom.	Gen.	Dat.	Acc.	Abl.
Masculine		Feminine		Neuter	

-um

	Singular		Plural		
CASE	(Nom.)	Gen.	Dat.	Acc.	Abl.
Masculine		Feminine		Neuter	

-a

	Singular		Plural		
CASE	Nom.	Gen.	Dat.	(Acc.)	Abl.
Masculine		Feminine		Neuter	

NOTE: Some of the correct choices have already been made for you. Can you make the additional choices necessary to complete the meal? This one is tricky!

Dessert:

Key Lime Pie
Double Chocolate Cherry Cake
French Silk Pie
Apple Cobbler
Spinach Pie

_____ (your favorite?)

mint

CHAPTER 11

lauNdRy day

<u>Robert</u> finished pulling up weeds in the backyard (his pants are hanging on the left). <u>Carolyn</u> just finished her soccer game (her shirt is hanging up on the right). And the <u>socks</u> need to be washed (neuter words)— phew! Draw lines from *masculine* words to Robert's jeans, from *feminine* words to Carolyn's shirt, and from *neuter* words to the washtub. Translate them as you go. We've done a few for you.

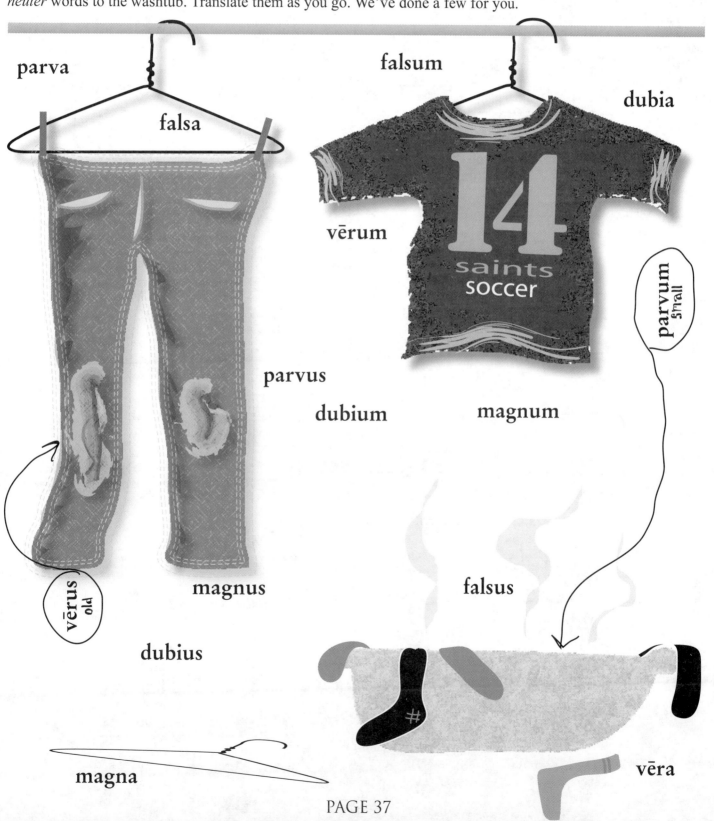

parva

falsa

falsum

dubia

vērum

parvus

dubium

magnum

parvum
small

magnus

falsus

dubius

vērus
old

magna

vēra

Chapter 12

Shoot the Moon

Word Crossing

When you get every one correct, that's called "shooting the moon." Can you do it?

14. friend (male)
17. I doubt
18. known
22. garden
24. gift
25. true
26. unknown

ACROSS
1. example
3. doubtful
5. old
7. miserable
9. angry
10. false
12. bad
13. I create

DOWN
2. I change
4. good
5. help

6. slave (male)
8. calm (or bright or clear)
11. happy
15. larger, great
16. I think
19. I explore
20. new
21. game
23. small

Can you get a hole in one?
By drawing a line, match the first- and second-declension adjectives
with their proper number, gender, and case; then it's off to the hole.

Mini Golf

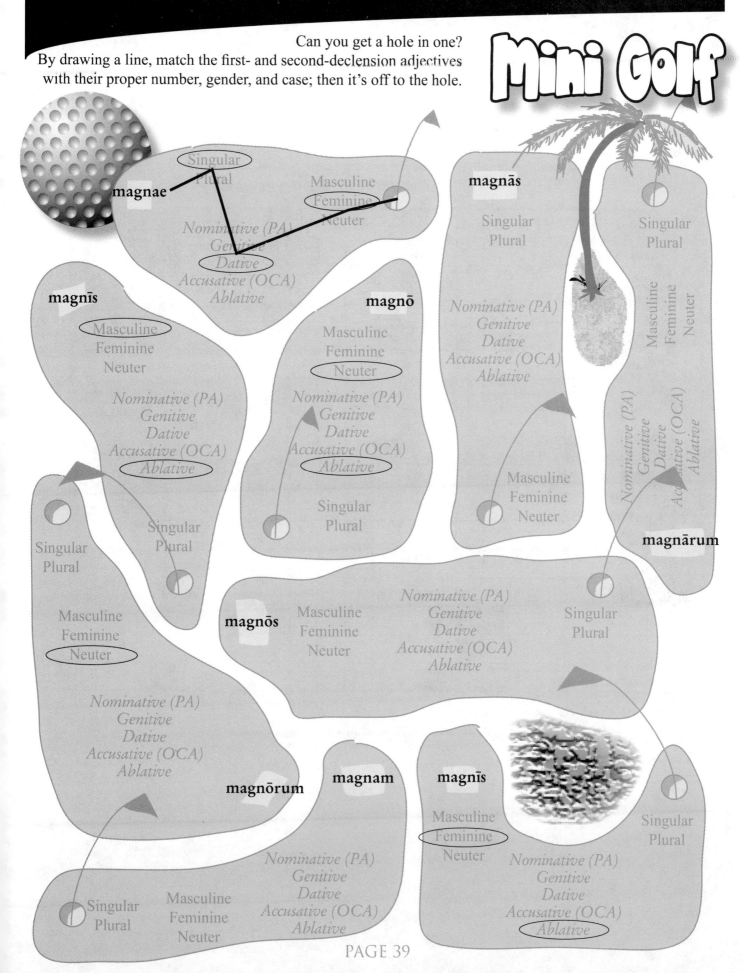

magnae

Singular
Plural

Masculine
Feminine
Neuter

Nominative (PA)
Genitive
Dative
Accusative (OCA)
Ablative

magnās

Singular
Plural

Nominative (PA)
Genitive
Dative
Accusative (OCA)
Ablative

Singular
Plural

Masculine
Feminine
Neuter

magnīs

Masculine
Feminine
Neuter

Nominative (PA)
Genitive
Dative
Accusative (OCA)
Ablative

Singular
Plural

magnō

Masculine
Feminine
Neuter

Nominative (PA)
Genitive
Dative
Accusative (OCA)
Ablative

Singular
Plural

Masculine
Feminine
Neuter

Nominative (PA)
Genitive
Dative
Accusative (OCA)
Ablative

magnārum

Singular
Plural

Nominative (PA)
Genitive
Dative
Accusative (OCA)
Ablative

Singular
Plural

Masculine
Feminine
Neuter

magnōs

Masculine
Feminine
Neuter

Nominative (PA)
Genitive
Dative
Accusative (OCA)
Ablative

Singular
Plural

Nominative (PA)
Genitive
Dative
Accusative (OCA)
Ablative

magnōrum

Masculine
Feminine
Neuter

magnam

Nominative (PA)
Genitive
Dative
Accusative (OCA)
Ablative

magnīs

Masculine
Feminine
Neuter

Nominative (PA)
Genitive
Dative
Accusative (OCA)
Ablative

Singular
Plural

Singular
Plural

Masculine
Feminine
Neuter

CHAPTER 12

Tricky Picky

Here's a tricky puzzle for you puzzle lovers! You have to fill the whole thing in—that's it. OK, we'll give you a little more help than that. Review this week's vocabulary words. The spaces below contain some of this week's words, but not all of them. By studying the amount of space provided on each line, can you figure out which Latin words are missing and their English translations? We've done the first one for you. Take your time and be patient.

b	o	n	u	s	,		g	o	o	d		(	m	)
		o			,							(		)
					,							(		)
	m					,						(		)
						,						(	n	)
					,	k	o				(		)
				,						(	f	)
					,						(	n	)
					,	n				(		)
					,		o				(	m	)
	t				,		o				(		)
					,		o	l	d		(	n	)
i				,				r			(	m	)
				,		h					(	n	)
		e	,				e			e		(	m	)
			,									(	)
			m	,								(	n	)

....

_____ _____ **sum.**

(I _____ _____ I am. —Descartes)

PAGE 40

REVIEW

Chapter 13

Back 2 Back

First Puzzle (upside down)

ACROSS
1. I shout
4. happy
5. I doubt
7. queen
9. false

DOWN
2. miserable
3. I change
5. doubtful
6. known
8. breeze

Second Puzzle

ACROSS
2. I create
4. old
8. small
9. unknown
11. good
12. angry
13. true

DOWN
1. bad
3. I explore
5. new
6. I think
7. larger, great
10. calm (or bright or clear)

PUZZLE IN
puzzle

OK, this maze is only for those who love 'em. Everyone else (yes, including you "mazers") should translate the English to Latin, then see how many of them you can find.

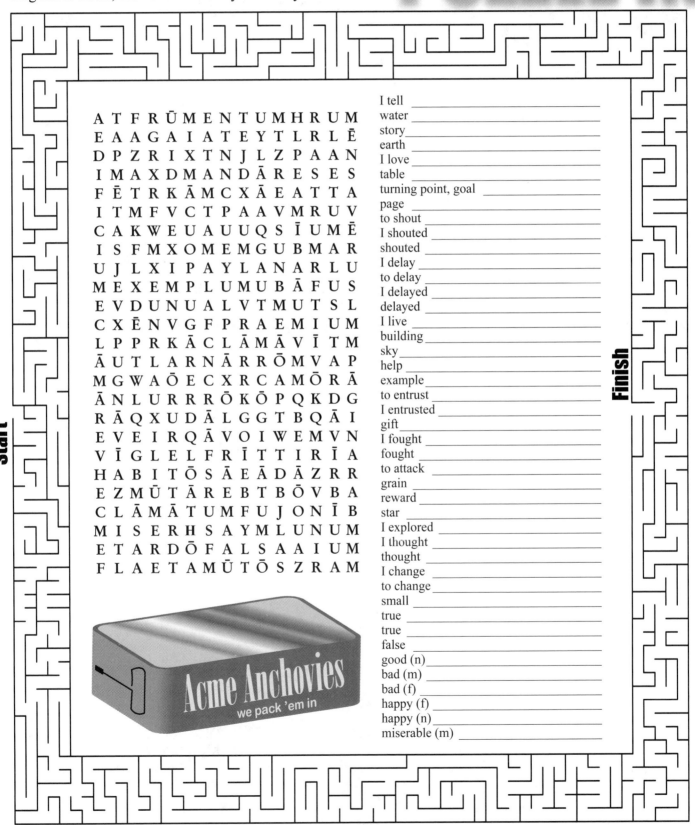

Start

Finish

```
A T F R Ū M E N T U M H R U M
E A A G A I A T E Y T L R L Ē
D P Z R I X T N J L Z P A A N
I M A X D M A N D Ā R E S E S
F Ē T R K Ā M C X Ā E A T T A
I T M F V C T P A A V M R U V
C A K W E U A U U Q S Ī U M Ē
I S F M X O M E M G U B M A R
U J L X I P A Y L A N A R L U
M E X E M P L U M U B Ā F U S
E V D U N U A L V T M U T S L
C X Ē N V G F P R A E M I U M
L P P R K Ā C L Ā M Ā V Ī T M
Ā U T L A R N Ā R R Ō M V A P
M G W A Ō E C X R C A M Ō R Ā
Ā N L U R R R Ō K Ō P Q K D G
R Ā Q X U D Ā L G G T B Q Ā I
E V E I R Q Ā V O I W E M V N
V Ī G L E L F R Ī T T I R Ī A
H A B I T Ō S Ā E Ā D Ā Z R R
E Z M Ū T Ā R E B T B Ō V B A
C L Ā M Ā T U M F U J O N Ī B
M I S E R H S A Y M L U N U M
E T A R D Ō F A L S A A I U M
F L A E T A M Ū T Ō S Z R A M
```

I tell _____
water _____
story _____
earth _____
I love _____
table _____
turning point, goal _____
page _____
to shout _____
I shouted _____
shouted _____
I delay _____
to delay _____
I delayed _____
delayed _____
I live _____
building _____
sky _____
help _____
example _____
to entrust _____
I entrusted _____
gift _____
I fought _____
fought _____
to attack _____
grain _____
reward _____
star _____
I explored _____
I thought _____
thought _____
I change _____
to change _____
small _____
true _____
true _____
false _____
good (n) _____
bad (m) _____
bad (f) _____
happy (f) _____
happy (n) _____
miserable (m) _____

Acme Anchovies
we pack 'em in

Spy Games!

Ahh, review! Can you unscramble these "old" Latin words, using the clues if necessary? Find the <u>two code phrases</u> that reveal the secrets of the puzzles.

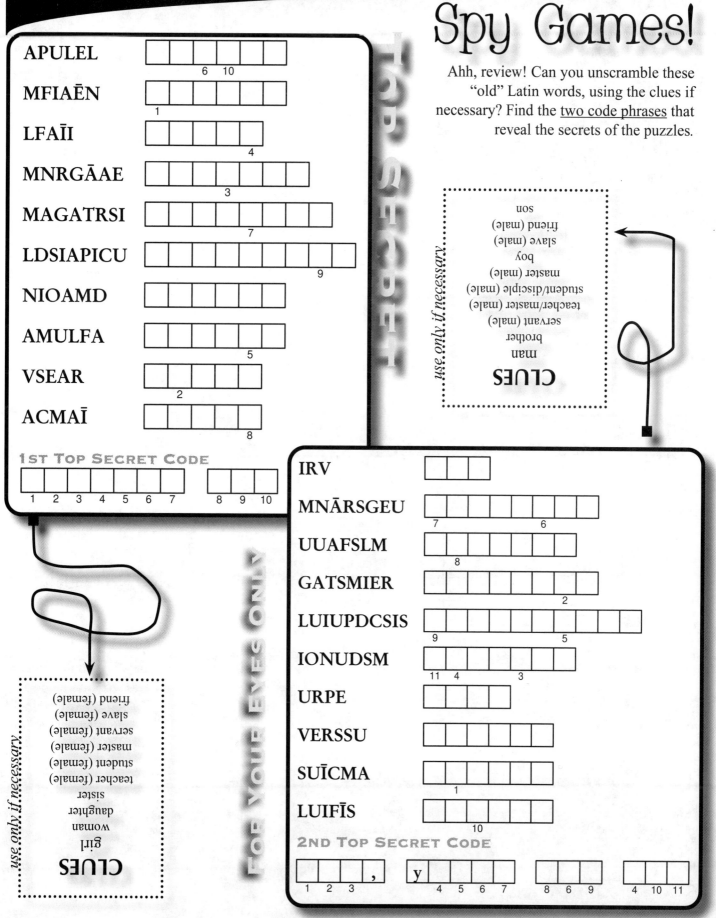

APULEL

MFIAĒN

LFAĪI

MNRGĀAE

MAGATRSI

LDSIAPICU

NIOAMD

AMULFA

VSEAR

ACMAĪ

1ST TOP SECRET CODE

| 1 | 2 | 3 | 4 | 5 | 6 | 7 | | 8 | 9 | 10 |

CLUES
use only if necessary

son
friend (male)
slave (male)
boy
master (male)
student/disciple (male)
teacher/master (male)
servant (male)
brother
man

FOR YOUR EYES ONLY

CLUES
use only if necessary

friend (female)
slave (female)
servant (female)
master (female)
student (female)
teacher (female)
sister
daughter
woman
girl

IRV

MNĀRSGEU

UUAFSLM

GATSMIER

LUIUPDCSIS

IONUDSM

URPE

VERSSU

SUĪCMA

LUIFĪS

2ND TOP SECRET CODE

| 1 | 2 | 3 | , | | y | 4 | 5 | 6 | 7 | | 8 | 6 | 9 | | 4 | 10 | 11 |

PAGE 43

Chapter 14

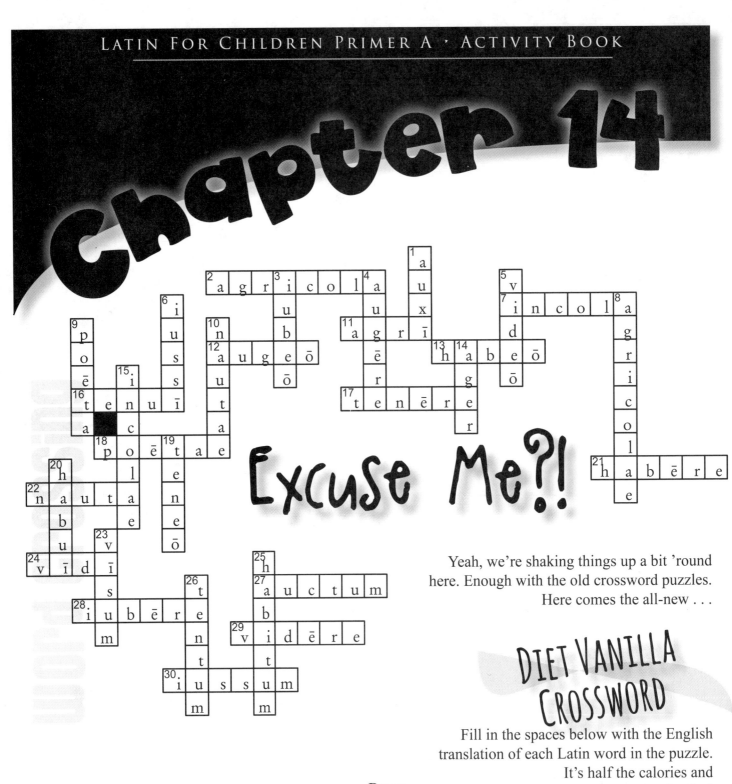

Excuse Me?!

Yeah, we're shaking things up a bit 'round here. Enough with the old crossword puzzles. Here comes the all-new . . .

DIET VANILLA CROSSWORD

Fill in the spaces below with the English translation of each Latin word in the puzzle. It's half the calories and twice the fun!

ACROSS

2. ___farmer___

7. _____

11. _____

12. _____

13. _____

16. _____

17. _____

18. _____

21. _____

22. _____

24. _____

27. _____

28. _____

29. _____

30. _____

DOWN

1. _____

3. _____

4. _____

5. _____

6. _____

8. _____

9. _____

10. _____

14. _____

15. _____

19. _____

20. _____

23. _____

25. _____

26. _____

Film & Videō

Lights! Cameras! Action!

Every good actor or actress needs the proper wardrobe to play the part. There are three actors here. Can you match the appropriate Latin word with the person and number (by drawing lines) so that everything is matched up?

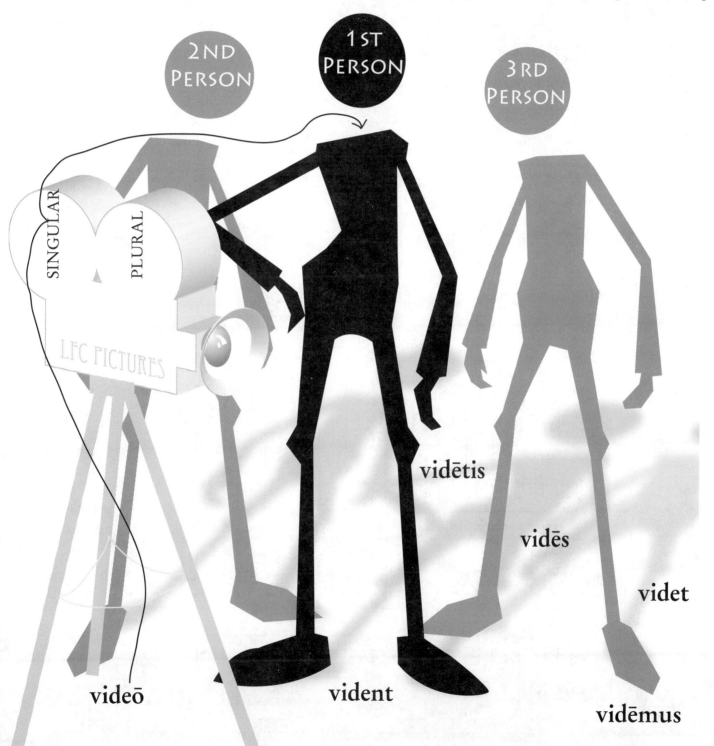

2ND PERSON

1ST PERSON

3RD PERSON

SINGULAR

PLURAL

LFC PICTURES

vidētis

vidēs

videt

videō

vident

vidēmus

While you're here, Director, would you mind translating these?

videō, vidēre, vīdī, vīsum _____, _____, _____, _____

CHAPTER 14

PYRAMID CLIMB

Finish

It's a big climb. Are you up for it?
Start at the bottom and collect the
Latin words as you go.

Three Latin words (then translate):

_____, _____

_____, _____

_____,

vidēre

vīsum

tenēre

poeta

augeō

habēre

incola

habitum

iussum

ager

auctum

auxī

tentum

agricola

Start

Chapter 15

Wild Fluvius

Well, it's more like a gentle stream. No matter. Can you paddle your way from the bottom to the top, filling in the spaces where needed, without getting all wet?

fluvii

river _____ wild animal

wind _____ horse

wind

ferus

food _____ horse

food _____ muri wall _____

_____ year _____ year

level space, plain, field _____ campus mind

animus _____ MIND

start

PAGE 47

ingredients

Below are two shopping lists. You'll need to look them over carefully. <u>Cross off the ingredients that you won't need.</u> <u>Put a checkmark beside those that you will need</u> in order to make the dishes (the sentences) labeled at the top of each list.

Pattern A Sentence

- ☒ Rubber ducky
- ☐ Swiss cheese
- ☐ Mustard—spicy!
- ☐ Subject noun
- ☐ A song and dance
- ☐ Orange juice with pulp
- ☐ A hammer and 16 nails
- ☐ A Latin book
- ☐ Simple form
- ☐ Ham
- ☐ Eggs
- ☐ Chocolate milk
- ☐ Pronoun
- ☐ X-Box
- ☐ Adjective
- ☐ Verb
- ☐ Predicate nominative
- ☐ Mailbox
- ☐ Accusative case
- ☐ Small rocks
- ☐ Subject verb
- ☐ SN
- ☐ Yellow marshmallow duckies
- ☐ V
- ☐ Green food coloring (for eggs above)
- ☐ PatA
- ☐ A new brother
- ☐ PB&J

Pattern B Sentence

- ☐ Small cow for hamburgers
- ☐ Hot dog buns
- ☐ Pattern for Suzie's skirt
- ☐ Linking verb
- ☐ Pool for the backyard
- ☐ Grill for Dad
- ☐ Pattern of "B"eing
- ☐ 1¾ nouns
- ☐ Extra-large LV
- ☐ PatB
- ☐ 2 lbs. pork chops
- ☐ Ablative
- ☐ Linking verb
- ☐ 3 nouns
- ☐ Cereal (ah, a little less sugar!)
- ☐ 2 nouns
- ☐ LV
- ☐ Spaghetti sauce
- ☐ SN
- ☐ PRN
- ☐ Predicate nominative
- ☐ Crackers (the good kind!)
- ☐ PRN nurse ($22/hr)
- ☐ Fruit (Is chocolate a fruit?)

finish

Box 1:
_____	mind
_____	year
_____	wind
_____	food
_____	river
_____	years

Box 2:
cibus	_____
plain	_____
_____	wall
_____	river
animī	_____
_____	wind

Box 3 (carrot):
campī	_____
ferī	_____
mūrī	level space
equus	_____

start

Track your way through the maze. When you come to a little "rabbit trail," translate what's in the box before moving on. Can you find your way to the end without missing any translations?

Rabbit Trails

Chapter 16

Across

1. I blow
2. I sailed
6. to call
7. I plowed
9. I call
11. sailed
13. to sail
15. to blow
16. of the gold
17. I avoided
18. of the silver
19. avoided
20. I sail

Down

1. I blew
3. called
4. of the arm
5. I plow
8. to avoid
10. plan
12. gold
14. silver
16. plowed
17. I called

_____ longa, _____ brevis.

(_____ *is long,* _____ *is brief.* —Seneca)

Jungle Jump!

We need someone brave enough to swing across these jungle vines. Can you do it?
You'll need to use what you've learned with the imperfect (past) verb endings by writing them
in at the bottom of the vines. You do still remember **-bam, -bās, -bat** . . . no?

Singular 2nd Person

Plural 3rd Person

Plural 1st Person

Singular 3rd Person

Plural 2nd Person

Singular 1st Person

JUNGLE ANTS!

Those pesky little buggers ate up our **amō, videō** table while
you were hanging around up above. Can you re-create the
table (fill it back in) from memory?

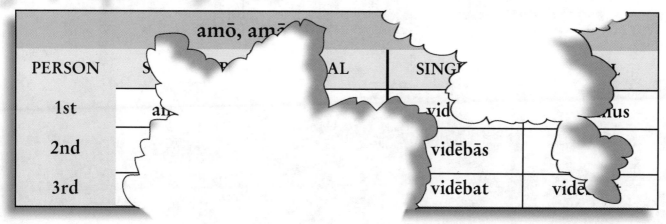

	amō, amā					
PERSON	S		AL	SING		
1st	a			vid		hus
2nd				vidēbās		
3rd				vidēbat		vid t

CHAPTER 16

Spider's Weavings

Ever wonder what it would be like to be a fly on the wall? Well, you're the fly, and you better get moving!

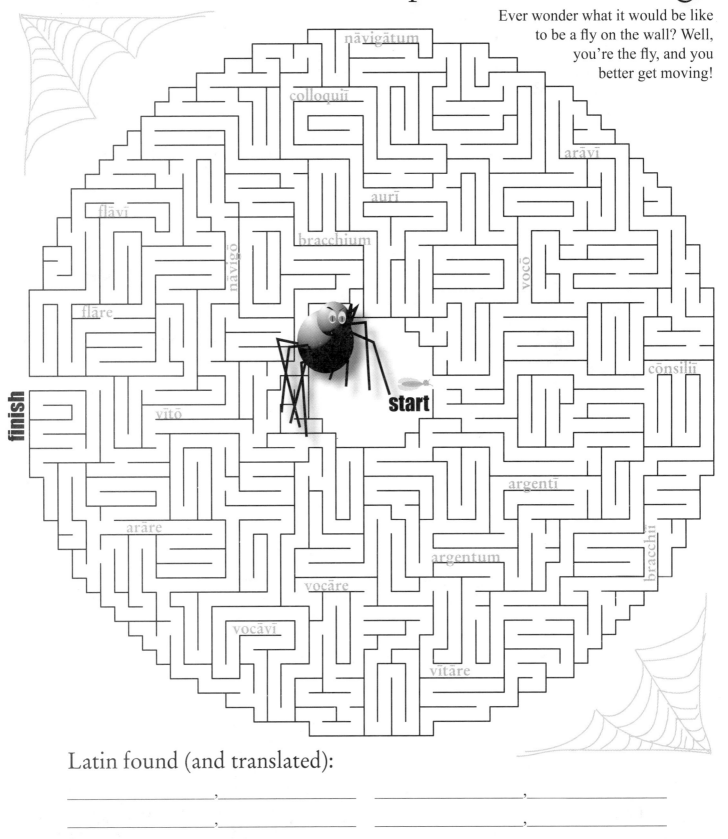

finish

start

nāvigātum

colloquiī

arāvī

aurī

flāvī

bracchium

nāvigō

voco

flāre

consiliī

vītō

argentī

arāre

bracchiī

argentum

vocāre

vocāvī

vītāre

Latin found (and translated):

_____,_____   _____,_____

_____,_____   _____,_____

_____,_____   _____,_____

Chapter 17

Busted!

Looks like someone dropped the word search and broke it. All of this week's words are in there somewhere. Can you still translate all the English into Latin and then find the Latin words?

iron _____

of iron _____

leaf _____

of leaf _____

monument _____

of monument _____

food for animals (fodder) _____

of food for animals (fodder) _____

rock _____

of rock _____

sign _____

of sign _____

silence _____

of silence _____

wall _____

of wall _____

sail _____

of sail _____

word _____

of word _____

```
S S S F R L Y W E H L P J R P
G K I O W K Z U E J V P F F R
B A I L M O N U M E N T Ī U L
S S B I E V Ē L U M M B C L V
Q I U U G N Y X L C I K H W N
O V G M N A T P Ā B U L Ī
Y Z I N E E I I M E B J P
D C R R Ī U X A U K P S I
U G M F C Z P M V M A
D A Q N N H A       G F
V E R B U M B
W P F A T L U
D N W P L J L
V Ē L Ī E W U
T   J K     O M
            C U
            Y U
```

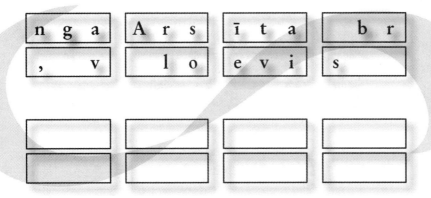

Tiles

Redraw the top tiles into the slots below to form a Latin phrase that you should know.

n g a	A r s	ī t a	b r
, v	l o	e v i s	s

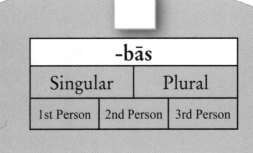

-bās		
Singular		Plural
1st Person	2nd Person	3rd Person

-bātis		
Singular		Plural
1st Person	2nd Person	3rd Person

-bāmus		
Singular		Plural
1st Person	2nd Person	3rd Person

You just knocked a ball *waaaaaay* out into left field. Can you run the bases successfully by circling the correct attributes of the imperfect verb endings and make it to home plate before they throw you out?

BATTER UP!

-bat		
1st Person	2nd Person	3rd Person

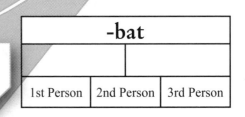

CRACK THE CODE

By now, you should be able to recall some of this week's vocabulary words from memory. Using the hints we've given you below, can you decode the message by finding each substitute letter?

A	B	C	D	E	F	G	H	I	J	K	L	M	N	O	P	Q	R	S	T	U	V	W	X	Y	Z
8																		10			21	20			

We've started this one for you. →

$$\overline{15}\ \overline{5}\ \overline{13}\ \overline{13}\ \overline{12}\ \overline{26}\ ,\ \overline{24}\ \overline{13}\ \overline{7}\ \overline{6}$$

$$\underset{10}{S}\ \underset{8}{A}\ \underset{20}{X}\ \bar{I}\ ,\ \overline{13}\ \overline{7}\ \overline{3}\ \overline{23}\ \text{(of)}$$

$$\overline{15}\ \overline{7}\ \overline{18}\ \overline{24}\ \overline{12}\ \overline{26}\ ,\ \overline{18}\ \overline{5}\ \overline{8}\ \overline{15}$$

$$\overline{26}\ \overline{7}\ \overline{6}\ \overline{12}\ \overline{26}\ \overline{5}\ \overline{6}\ \overline{25}\ \overline{12}\ \overline{26}\ ,\ \overline{26}\ \overline{7}\ \overline{6}\ \overline{12}\ \overline{26}\ \overline{5}\ \overline{6}\ \overline{25}$$

$$\overline{22}\ \overline{5}\ \overline{13}\ \overline{19}\ \overline{12}\ \overline{26}\ ,\ \overset{W}{\overline{21}}\ \overline{7}\ \overline{13}\ \overline{17}$$

$$\overline{22}\ \overline{8}\ \overline{18}\ \overline{18}\ \bar{I}\ ,\ \overset{W}{\overline{21}}\ \overline{8}\ \overline{18}\ \overline{18}$$

$$\overline{26}\ \overline{7}\ \overline{6}\ \overline{12}\ \overline{26}\ \overline{5}\ \overline{6}\ \overline{25}\ \bar{I}\ ,\ \overline{26}\ \overline{7}\ \overline{6}\ \overline{12}\ \overline{26}\ \overline{5}\ \overline{6}\ \overline{25}\ \text{(of)}$$

$$\overline{4}\ \overline{8}\ \overline{19}\ \overline{12}\ \overline{18}\ ^-\ \bar{I}\ ,\ \overline{15}\ \overline{7}\ \overline{7}\ \overline{17}\ \overline{15}\ \overline{7}\ \overline{13}\ \overline{8}\ \overline{6}\ \overline{24}\ \overline{26}\ \overline{8}\ \overline{18}\ \overline{10}$$

$$\overline{10}\ \overline{8}\ \overline{20}\ \overline{12}\ \overline{26}\ ,\ \overline{13}\ \overline{7}\ \overline{3}\ \overline{23}$$

$$\overline{10}\ \overline{24}\ \overline{18}\ \overline{5}\ \overline{6}\ \overline{25}\ \overline{24}\ \bar{I}\ ,\ \overline{10}\ \overline{24}\ \overline{18}\ \overline{5}\ \overline{6}\ \overline{3}\ \overline{5}\ \text{(of)}$$

$$\overline{10}\ \overline{24}\ \overline{18}\ \overline{5}\ \overline{6}\ \overline{25}\ \overline{24}\ \overline{12}\ \overline{26}\ ,\ \overline{10}\ \overline{24}\ \overline{18}\ \overline{5}\ \overline{6}\ \overline{3}\ \overline{5}$$

$$\overline{22}\ \overline{8}\ \overline{18}\ \overline{18}\ \overline{12}\ \overline{26}\ ,\ \overset{W}{\overline{21}}\ \overline{8}\ \overline{18}\ \overline{18}$$

$$\overline{4}\ \overline{8}\ \overline{19}\ \overline{12}\ \overline{18}\ \overline{12}\ \overline{26}\ ,\ \overline{15}\ \overline{7}\ \overline{7}\ \overline{17}\ \overline{15}\ \overline{7}\ \overline{13}\ \overline{8}\ \overline{6}\ \overline{24}\ \overline{26}\ \overline{8}\ \overline{18}\ \overline{10}$$

$$\overline{10}\ \overline{24}\ \overline{9}\ \overline{6}\ \bar{I}\ ,\ \overline{10}\ \overline{24}\ \overline{9}\ \overline{6}\ \text{(of)}$$

$$\overline{22}\ \overline{5}\ \overline{18}\ ^-\ \bar{I}\ ,\ \overline{10}\ \overline{8}\ \overline{24}\ \overline{18}$$

$$\overline{22}\ \overline{5}\ \overline{13}\ \overline{19}\ \bar{I}\ ,\ \overset{W}{\overline{21}}\ \overline{7}\ \overline{13}\ \overline{17}\ \text{(of)}$$

$$\overline{15}\ \overline{7}\ \overline{18}\ \overline{24}\ \bar{I}\ ,\ \overline{18}\ \overline{5}\ \overline{8}\ \overline{15}$$

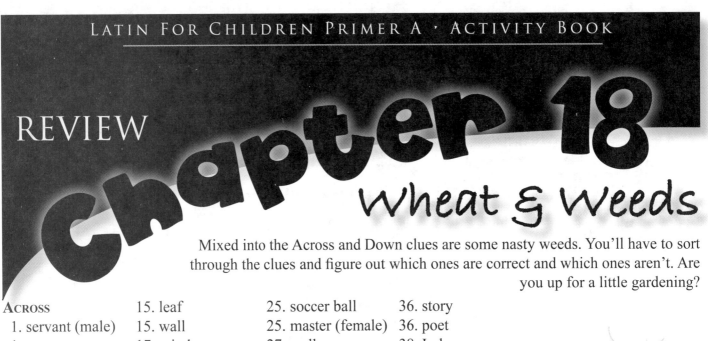

REVIEW Chapter 18
Wheat & Weeds

Mixed into the Across and Down clues are some nasty weeds. You'll have to sort through the clues and figure out which ones are correct and which ones aren't. Are you up for a little gardening?

ACROSS

1. servant (male)
1. poet
4. story
6. arm
6. leg
11. word
11. mind
12. I call
15. leaf
15. wall
17. mind
18. monument
19. sailor
19. I plow
20. I have
21. farmer
23. I hold
25. soccer ball
25. master (female)
27. wall
29. leaf
29. leaf blower
30. son
31. wild animal
34. teacher/master (male)
36. story
36. poet
38. I plow
39. food
43. food for animals (fodder)
44. sail
45. building
47. year

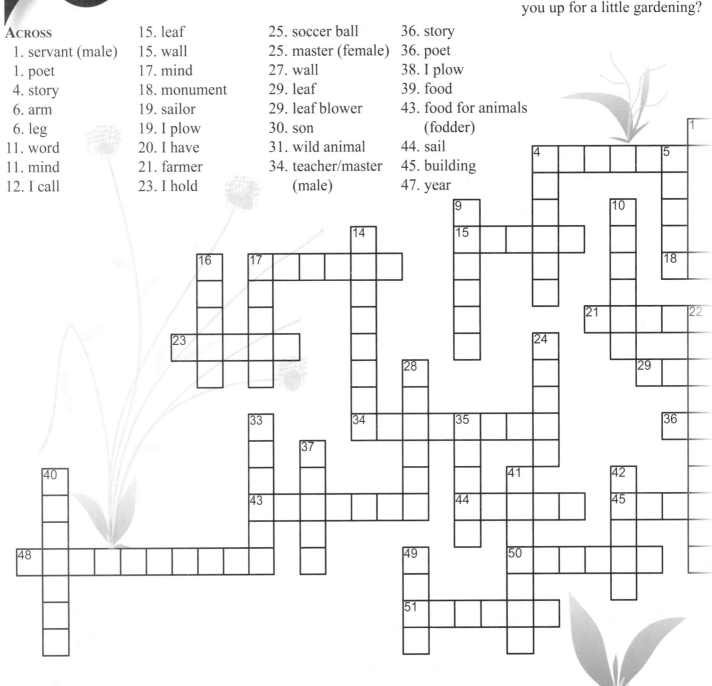

48. student/disciple (male)
50. wind
51. fly a kite
51. sky
52. I blow

DOWN
2. field
3. silence
4. water
4. servant (female)
5. gold
5. silver
7. silver
8. friend (female)

9. I walk
10. I sail
10. more help
12. I avoid
13. plan
14. iron horse
14. help
16. I see
16. rock
17. I increase
22. conversation
24. I tell
26. water
26. settler
28. sign

30. iron
32. horse
32. rocking horse
33. level space, plain, field
35. slave (female)
37. I order
37. Chinese takeout
40. river
40. master (male)
41. river
42. rock
42. help
46. settler
49. I kill

CHAPTER 18

MATCH A BATCH

Draw lines to match the correct verb with its English derivative.

videō	tenacious
teneō	vocal, vocation
habeō	habitat, habitation (where one lives), habit
iubeō	no derivatives
augeō	arable (fit for farming)
arō	video (movie), vision
nāvigō	navigate, navigation, navigator
vocō	augment, augmentation

BATCH A MATCH

Draw lines to match the correct noun with its English derivative.

ferus	annual
nauta, -ae	silent, silence
silentium, -ī	animate, animated (spirited, moving)
ager, -ī	poet, poetry
equus, -ī	camp, campus
poēta, -ae	verb, verbal, verbose (using a lot of words)
campus, -ī	foliate, foliage
folium, -ī	feral (wild), ferocious
annus, -ī	nautical (relating to seamen, ships, or navigation)
mūrus, -ī	mural
animus, -ī	equestrian
verbum, -ī	agriculture

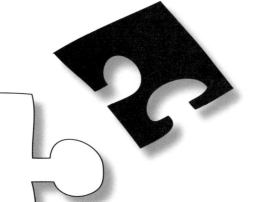

Chapter 19
HOT LAVA!
It's smokin'!

You have to jump across from rock to rock (in order) without using the rocks with incorrect Latin, which will only crumble underfoot. Can you cross the lava field without getting scorched?

start

exercēre
to exercise

dolēre
to suffer

capillī
to cap (as on
a bottle)

gaudēre
to rejoice

iacēre
to lie down

deī
to diet
(unsuccessfully)

capillus
hair

humī
of earth,
ground, land

locus
place

exerceō
I train

dolitūrus
I rejoice

cāvī
I guarded
against

locī
crazy
(like a younger sibling)

finish

Invasion!

Aliens are landing!

Can you help our visiting aliens connect with the correct Latin and practice your future verb endings at the same time? Connect all three parts by drawing lines between the correct parts!

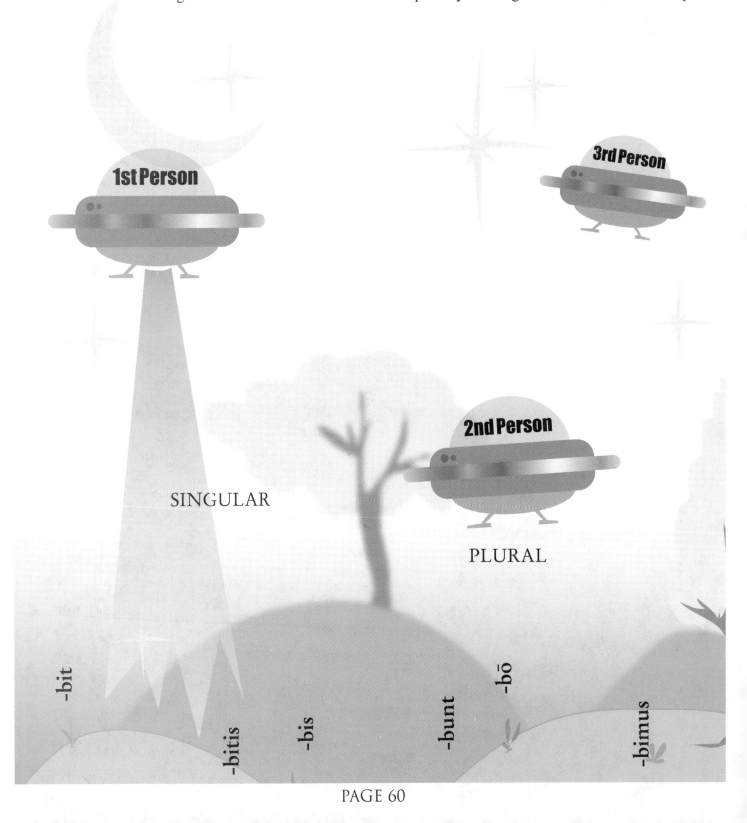

1st Person

3rd Person

2nd Person

SINGULAR

PLURAL

-bit

-bitis

-bis

-bunt

-bō

-bimus

NORTH AMERICA

EUROPE

The Great Swim!

1	t o
2	e	s
3	u t	.
4	d s
5	s h o
6	i l e
7	e x t
8	n	t
9	z z l
10	n t	,
11	t h e
12	e y

13	e
(14)	W h e
15	i s
16	w o r
17	u t
18	r a
19	h e y
20	T h
21	a r
22	t h
23	p u
24	l o
25	i s
26	f i l

Can you swim all the way across the Atlantic Ocean? Start the maze and collect the numbers as you go by circling them in the center column. The numbers you collect will tell you which tiles to use as you figure out the phrase below. Swim hard and don't give up!

start

finish

| W h e | | | | | | | |
| | | | | | | | |

Translate this phrase into Latin: _____

_____

Chapter 20

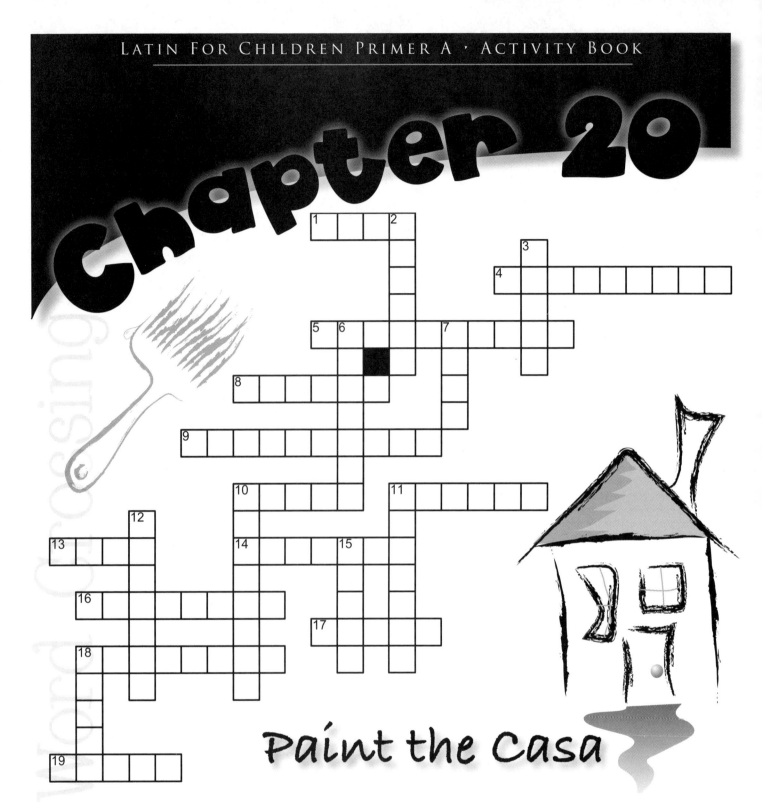

Paint the Casa

Want to help paint the house? Fill out the crossword puzzle and you will have given it a fresh new coat!

ACROSS

1. god
4. heading, chapter
5. tomb
8. I rejoice
9. benefit
10. I guard against
11. roof
13. rumor, report, fame
14. food for animals (fodder)
16. letter
17. earth, ground, land
18. enemy (personal)
19. I suffer

DOWN

2. sign
3. rock
6. I train
7. house
10. hair
11. temple
12. family
15. place
18. I lie down

CHAPTER 20

MESSAGE IN THE BOTTLE

Oooo, look what floated ashore! Can you fill in the boxes to complete the accusative endings?

NEUTER

2ND DEC.

Nom.	
	-ō
	-a
Abl.	

1ST DEC.

Nom.	
	-a
Dat.	
Abl.	-am
	-ae
Dat.	
	-īs

MASC.

2ND DEC.

	-us
Gen.	-ī
Gen.	-ōrum

CHAPTER 20

Safe Cracker!

The government needs you! Foreign spies have captured top-secret documents. Can you crack the safe by using all of your Latin skills (vocabulary from this week and review) to fill in the spaces and recover the documents?

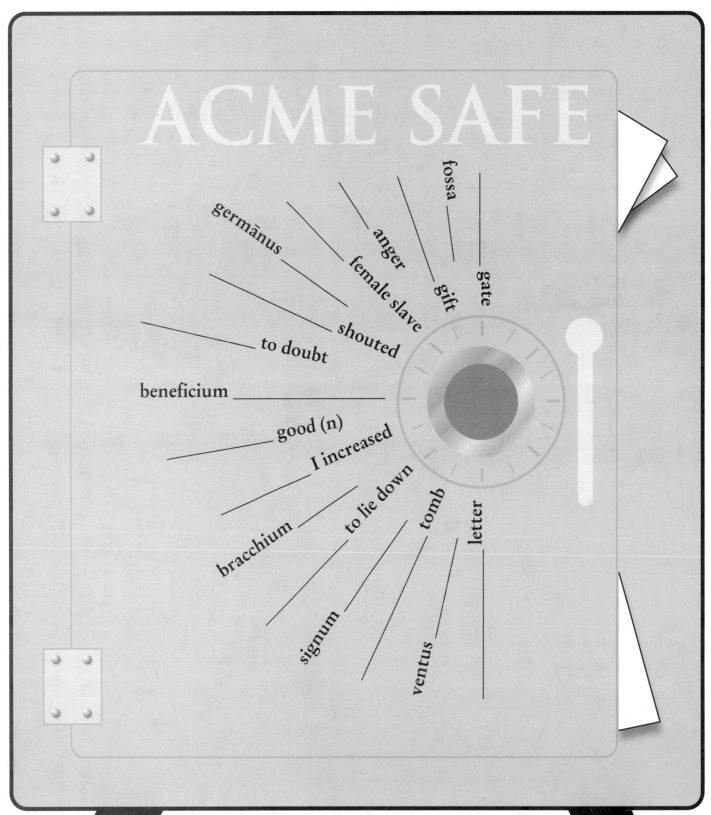

ACME SAFE

fossa _____

anger _____

female slave _____

gift _____

gate _____

germānus _____

to doubt _____

shouted _____

beneficium _____

good (n) _____

I increased _____

bracchium _____

to lie down _____

tomb _____

letter _____

signum _____

ventus _____

Chapter 21

The crossword grid contains the following entries:

Across:
- 4. audeō
- 6. cēnsēre
- 7. dignus
- 10. cāra
- 11. longum
- 14. audēre
- 15. manēre
- 17. parāta
- 19. clāra
- 20. censuī
- 21. cārus
- 22. clārum

Down:
- 1. laugeō (lūgeō)
- 2. cēnseō
- 3. longus
- 5. longa
- 7. digna
- 8. dignum
- 9. longō
- 12. monēre
- 13. parātārum
- 15. monitī
- 16. mantuō (mantuō)
- 17. parātam
- 18. mānsī
- 23. lūxī

Note: If two words intersect but only one has a macron at the intersection, that macron is not shown.

DIET LEMON CROSSWORD

That's right, folks! It's time to put a spin on the ole crossword puzzle.
Can you fill in the English translations?

Across

4. _____
6. _____
7. _____
10. _____
11. _____
14. _____
15. _____
17. _____
19. _____
20. _____
21. _____
22. _____

Down

1. _____
2. _____
3. _____
5. _____
7. _____
8. _____
9. _____
10. _____
12. _____
13. _____
15. _____
16. _____
17. _____
18. _____
23. _____

Petal Pushers

Can you cross out the incorrect petals that don't match with the flower's center?

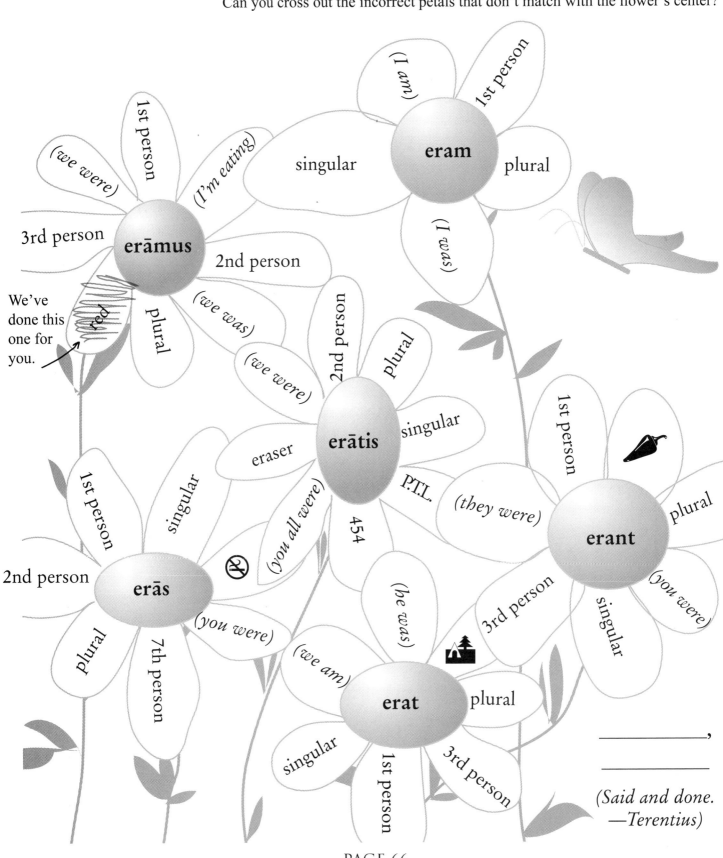

eram — (I am) / 1st person / singular / plural / (I was)

erāmus — (we were) / 1st person / (I'm eating) / 3rd person / 2nd person / plural / (we was) / (we were)

We've done this one for you. → red

erātis — 2nd person / plural / singular / eraser / P.T.L. / (you all were) / 454

erās — 1st person / singular / 2nd person / plural / 7th person / (you were)

erant — 1st person / plural / (they were) / 3rd person / singular / (you were)

erat — (we am) / (he was) / plural / singular / 1st person / 3rd person

_____,
_____
*(Said and done.
—Terentius)*

CHAPTER 21

BIRDS OF A FEATHER

Slowly climb the pole and make it all the way to the birdhouse on top, filling in the spaces as you go.
Then you can set about finding those Latin words within the puzzle.

```
C R M X L B L R K R J V G J Z H C H A A
A Y Z G M B K D S F N C E P V C W U G U
R Q X Q F V W L K I P S F P A R Ā T U S
W S L Q B E E L O N G A U D Ē R E R B U
E X D C N T D I G N U S R C C L Ā R U S
D P O F H Q D K X P G C L Ā R U M T I S
G S M W B I U D I G N U M R T O O G U U
A E N M M R P S G C Ē N S U M A N S U M
B N Y A P P V J V H S S V M O Z E R A O
V L E B M H L M A U V J M A N E Ō Z Z N
E V J V A L L E M E I P C P Ū I Y E G I
Y P C G W H C G G G M Ā N S Ī L E M L T
H J F S M C I I T B K X C W M A Ū S P U
Y Y M B S U W K J V V J H D L O N G U M
D D Y F W D Q J D M H S G Y S Ū A T E J
X K D X Q L M U N M O H A F A Z X U O Ō
B B O R W D R I C G N M Q W W A P Ī P J
Z R Q O U M X Z V O G P J B S K M M M H
M P R F O X N R L X Z E O A I F L Q C L
E E J C H X C L W L X X V C B L B S B H
C D I G N A A I I A I H C A U T J M T C
A L Ū C T U M R A A B I V J Z Y N J G R
W W Ū H E D O P C M F Z O K S W C P A T
I F I G C Ē N S E Ō M I E S Q K P U T J
D F M C Ē Ō Ē J U B E Q U C D T U A S F
C L A R Ā R R U Z G W Q M Z H S K B S V
C Ē N S Ē R E J L S J I G R R G E Z R K
H A Ē V P C A U E R S L U M O L L V X M
J Y R Z J Q W I D G N E Q A O F E J V V
M C Ē N S U Ī L X A X N Y E U T S V J W
```

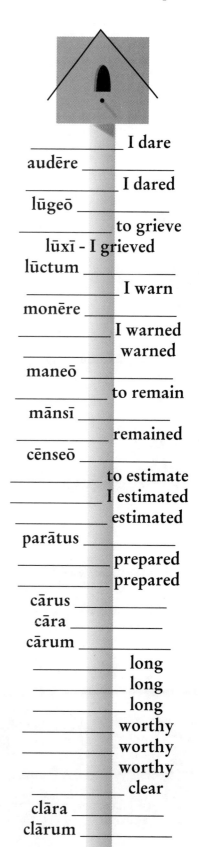

_____ I dare
audēre _____
_____ I dared
lūgeō _____
_____ to grieve
lūxī - I grieved
lūctum _____
_____ I warn
monēre _____
_____ I warned
_____ warned
maneō _____
_____ to remain
mānsī _____
_____ remained
cēnseō _____
_____ to estimate
_____ I estimated
_____ estimated
parātus _____
_____ prepared
_____ prepared
cārus _____
cāra _____
cārum _____
_____ long
_____ long
_____ long
_____ worthy
_____ worthy
_____ worthy
_____ clear
clāra _____
clārum _____

Chapter 22

BLOCK PARTY!

Sure, these can be a bit tricky, but with all the hints we've given you and the fact that we're letting you use your book, you should do just fine.

But first, how many of this week's vocabulary words can you fill in *without* looking at your book?

Behind the 8 Ball

Each Latin ball (present and imperfect of **sum**) needs to bounce between all of its correct components. Use colored pencils to draw a line bouncing each ball off its correct sidewall, then into its correct hole. Are you a pool shark?

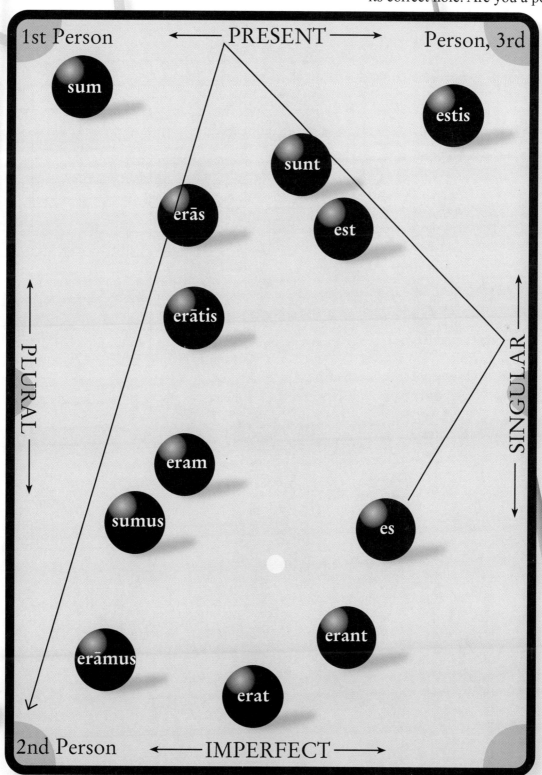

CHAPTER 22

Word Crossing

Rebuilding Rome

Rome burned in AD 476. Can you help rebuild this coliseum that's fallen over?

ACROSS
2. long
4. I train
7. prepared
9. cowardly
10. clear
13. I lie down
14. I suffer
15. place
16. strange, wonderful
17. grateful
19. tired
20. horrendous
21. I remain
22. just

DOWN
1. I dare
2. I grieve
3. hair
5. I estimate
6. blind
8. silent
9. enemy (personal)
10. I guard against
11. worthy
12. dirty
14. god
15. broad
16. I warn
17. I rejoice
18. dear

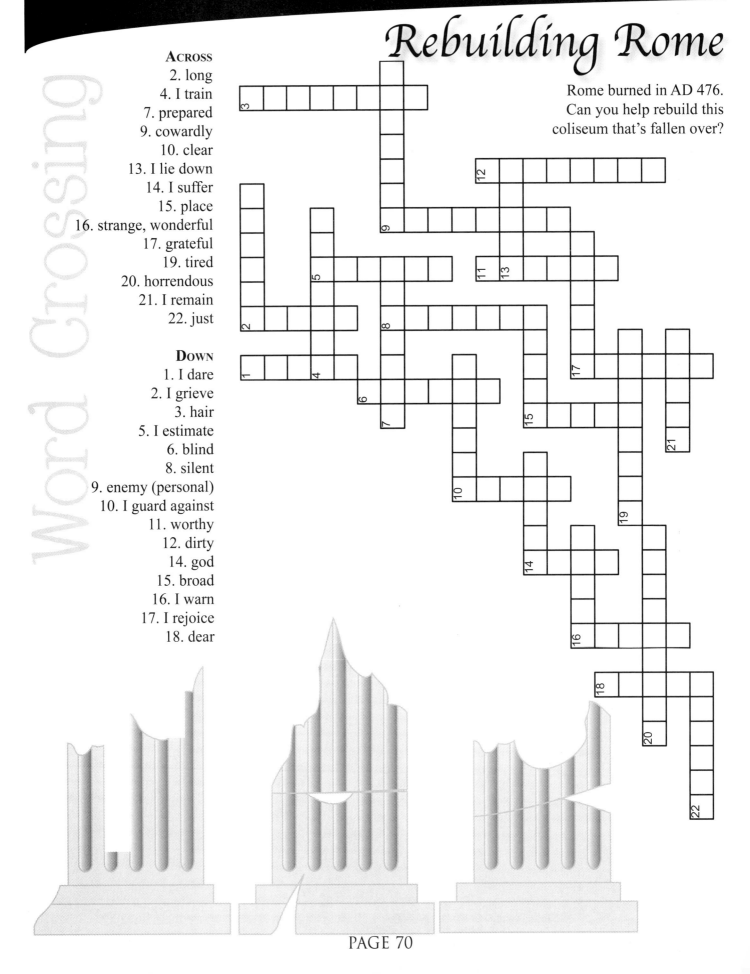

REVIEW

Chapter 23

Look what the cat dragged in!
You'll have to keep on your toes in order to finish this one.
And remember, don't blow your top!

A
WHALE
OF A
PUZZLE!

CONTINUED . . .

(N, G, D, A, A)
What does this mean?
_____
_____
_____

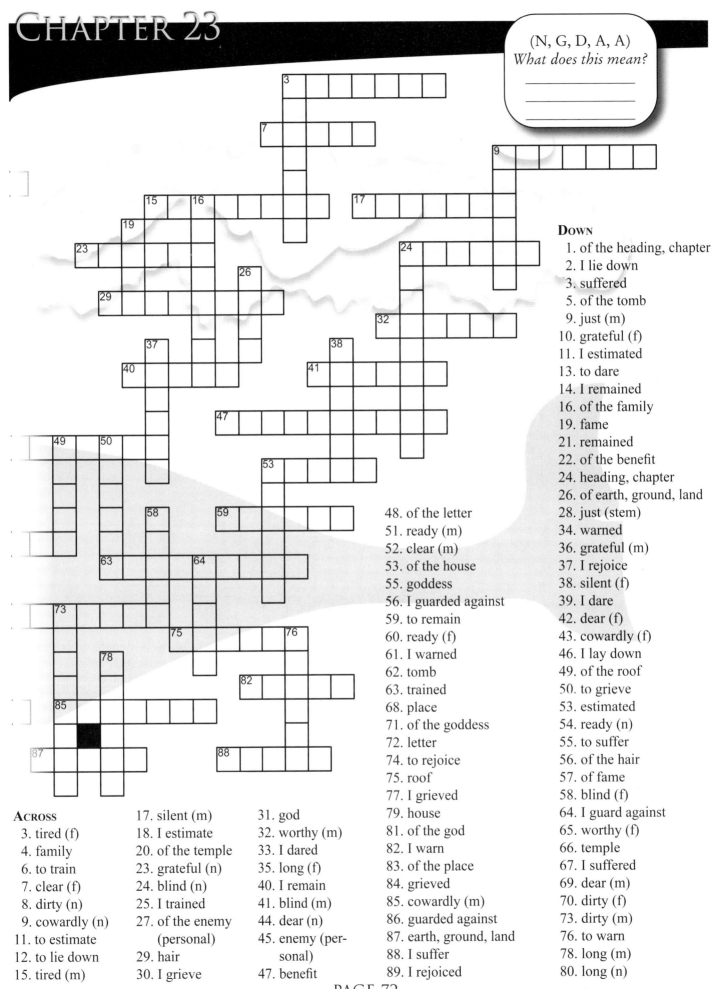

DOWN

1. of the heading, chapter
2. I lie down
3. suffered
5. of the tomb
9. just (m)
10. grateful (f)
11. I estimated
13. to dare
14. I remained
16. of the family
19. fame
21. remained
22. of the benefit
24. heading, chapter
26. of earth, ground, land
28. just (stem)
34. warned
36. grateful (m)
37. I rejoice
38. silent (f)
39. I dare
42. dear (f)
43. cowardly (f)
46. I lay down
49. of the roof
50. to grieve
53. estimated
54. ready (n)
55. to suffer
56. of the hair
57. of fame
58. blind (f)
64. I guard against
65. worthy (f)
66. temple
67. I suffered
69. dear (m)
70. dirty (f)
73. dirty (m)
76. to warn
78. long (m)
80. long (n)

48. of the letter
51. ready (m)
52. clear (m)
53. of the house
55. goddess
56. I guarded against
59. to remain
60. ready (f)
61. I warned
62. tomb
63. trained
68. place
71. of the goddess
72. letter
74. to rejoice
75. roof
77. I grieved
79. house
81. of the god
82. I warn
83. of the place
84. grieved
85. cowardly (m)
86. guarded against
87. earth, ground, land
88. I suffer
89. I rejoiced

ACROSS

3. tired (f)
4. family
6. to train
7. clear (f)
8. dirty (n)
9. cowardly (n)
11. to estimate
12. to lie down
15. tired (m)
17. silent (m)
18. I estimate
20. of the temple
23. grateful (n)
24. blind (n)
25. I trained
27. of the enemy (personal)
29. hair
30. I grieve
31. god
32. worthy (m)
33. I dared
35. long (f)
40. I remain
41. blind (m)
44. dear (n)
45. enemy (personal)
47. benefit

M●MA
(Museum of Modern Art)

Pull out your paintbrushes, your colored markers, and your glitter. It's time to make art!
Do you know your Latin well enough to sketch these paintings?

capillus on the casa

familia cāra

sordidus locus

epistula longa

tēctum templī

caecus vir

horrendum sepulchrum

puella luget

Chapter 24
CAPED CRUSADER

This city is in need of a good superhero. Up for the challenge? You must fly about and rescue the Latin words (future tense of **sum**) from the burning building and drop them off with the correct ambulance. Using colored pens, draw a line from our hero to the Latin word, then to its translation, and last to its person.

you all will be

singular

you will be

erunt

erō

erit

he, she, or it will be

eritis

they will be

eris

plural

I will be

erimus

we will be

3rd Person

2nd Person

1st Person

Postal Delivery

Rain or shine, the mail must go through! Deliver the mail, translating out loud as you go.

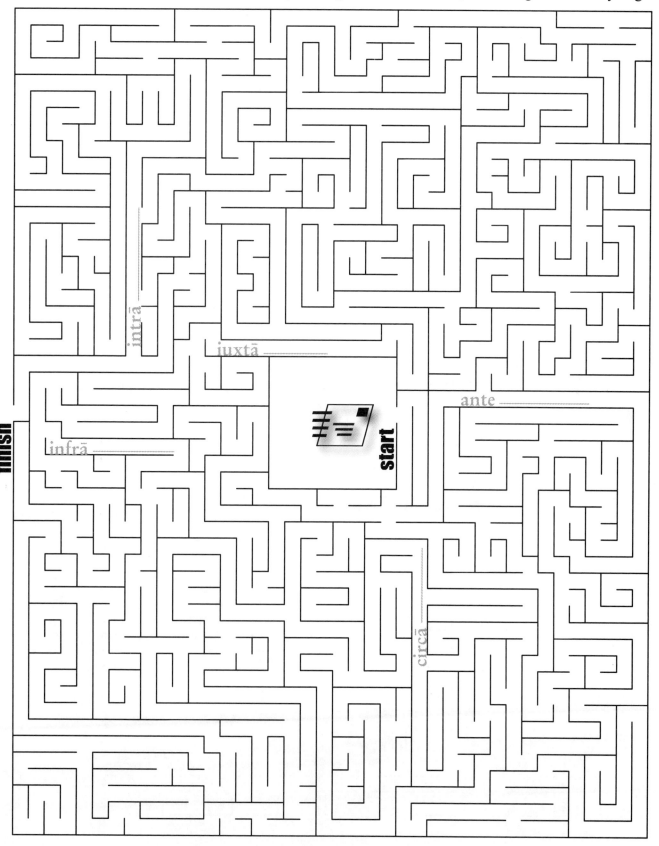

Short Order

Can you unscramble these words? Use the clues below for help.

RŌTIN

SOASF
1

SEATNFER
7

MĒFIAEN
3

IUONMSD
4

ĪĀĒSNŌTMRVD
6

ĀPNMUGTU
10

CUOLML
13 9

ĀUMTMŪT

TNAŌ
2

AUNAT
12

ŪUSMR
8

VTUTĪMĀ

EMĪTONMNU
11

ĪUOLD

DEEA
15

RTPĀSAU
5

ARĀGT

TNAE
14

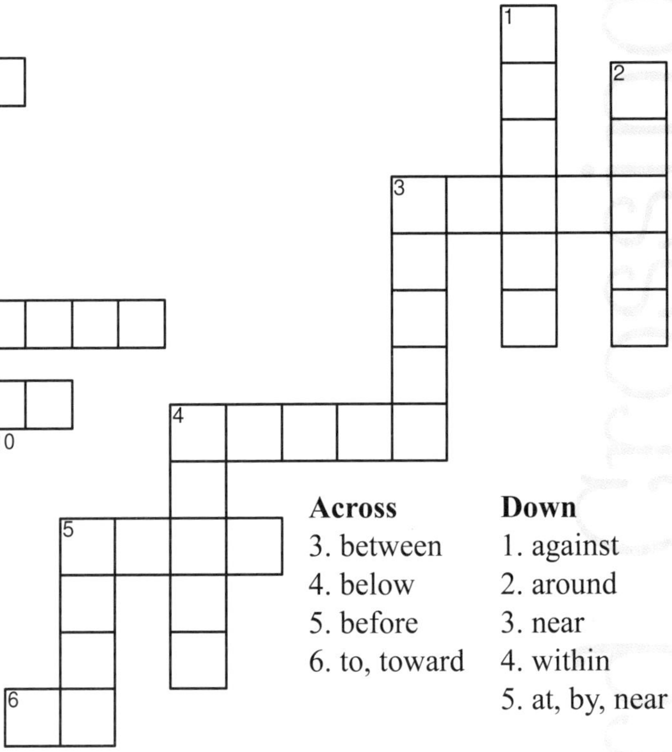

Across
3. between
4. below
5. before
6. to, toward

Down
1. against
2. around
3. near
4. within
5. at, by, near

Short & Sweet

clues

I enter
ditch
window
woman
master (male)
I pointed out
fought
neck
changed
known (f)

sailor
wall
avoided
monument
I suffered
goddess
prepared
grateful
before

HINT: "AN OBSERVATION"

| 1 | 2 | 3 | | w | 5 | 6 | | 7 | 8 | 9 | 10 | | 11 | 12 | 13 h | | w | 14 | k 15 |

Chapter 25

GO WITH THE FLOW

_____, beyond

Can you navigate your way around this diagram? Fill in the blanks for this accusative preposition flowchart.

_____, across

_____, around

_____, over, above, on top of

_____, in front of

_____, over, above, beyond

_____, before

, past

_____, after

_____, through

_____, along

, within

between

_____, near
_____, near

_____, outside of

, below

_____, on account of

, against

_____, to, toward

+

_____, with, near

a b c

_____, _____

(By _____, we learn. —Seneca)

CHAPTER 25

Staircase

Up and down, up and down!
Venture into the first maze and collect the <u>three</u> English words as you go. Write them in and translate them (on the steps). Then collect the Latin words buried in the second maze and do the same underneath.

Start

Finish

star

after

near

north

across

beyond

beyond

Latin , Translation

Latin , Translation

praeter

peanut butter

super

post

along

supra

ultra

per

Latin , Translation

Latin , Translation

ob

propter

Latin , Translation

Latin , Translation

CHAPTER 25

MAN IN THE MOON

They say that the moon is made of Swiss cheese. That may be true, especially if you look at this puzzle. There are holes not only all over the crossword puzzle but also in the questions. With the hints we've given you, along with the fact that all of the moon's questions are prepositions (which take the accusative case), can you slowly fill in everything else? Use your textbook if you must.

Across 1. near 2. bElow 3.

WE'VE DONE THIS ONE FOR you.

12. near 13. _____

8.

5. beyond 6.

2.

17. on account of **Down 1.**

4.

7. after 9.

10.

16.

11. across 13.

14. over, above, beyond 15.

Puzzle letters filled in: x, n, r, o, t, u, r, a, s, ā, u, c, t, n, u, r, p, a, e, t, r

REVIEW

Chapter 26

Boxed In!

Fill in the boxes!
It's your only way out.

IMPERFECT

_____	_____ _I was_
____ person	_____
____ person	**erat** _____

_____	**erō** _____
1st _____	
_____	**eris** _____
3rd person	**erit** _____

_____	
1st _____	**eramus** _____
2nd person	_____
____ person	_____ _they were_

PRESENT

____ person	_____ _I am_
____ person	_____
	_____ _he is_

_____	
_____	_____ _we are_
2nd person	_____ _you all are_
3rd _____	_____

FUTURE

____ person	_____ _we will be_
2nd _____	_____
3rd _____	**erunt** _____

CHAPTER 26

The Big Race!

74 Add, address

08 Antebellum, antecedent, anteroom

88 No derivatives

66 Circus, circle, circulate

61 Contrary, contradict

19 Extraordinary, extraterrestrial

21 Infrared, infrastructure

39 Interest, intersperse, interact

51 Introvert, intravenous

12 Juxtapose, juxtaposition

48 Observe, oblong, obsess

66 Perfect, per chance, perennial

04 Preternatural

93 Propinquity

91 Second, secondary

38 Supersonic, supercharge, supercomputer

56 Supranational

18 Transfer, transform, transact

Every good auto racer knows their car has to have a racing number on its hood. That's how the spectators can tell the cars apart. Can you put the derivative's racing numbers on the correct hoods (containing the Latin roots)?

infrā 21

WE'VE DONE THIS ONE FOR YOU.

iuxtā

circā

secundum

33

prope

extrā

inter

super

contrā

ad

trāns

apud

intrā

ob

suprā

ante

praeter

per

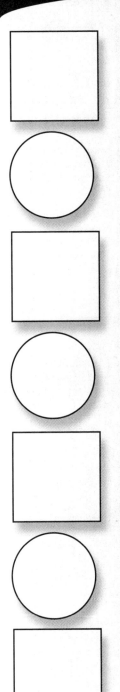

```
A F T E R M A K B I U J P I J F B C R N
R O X D B C Q H V E I N Z X D J E I A A
I M K T O D Z L K C Y Y P C O X F R W P
O N B E T W E E N P R O P T E R O C I U
S W T U Y N S X W I T I N T E R R Ā T D
Y U D R Z W O E T U A H E D H A E O H P
R S P A Ā V V M C U L T R Ā O Z P U I O
A G G R O B E F I U O A R O U N D T N S
Q N G U Ā N R J O Q N O R X U B B S V T
N V T R L J A H B D G D C X C G T I G T
Y E F E T B B C W D E S U Q D Q H D G N
B Z A U R D O G C F G N W M D K K E J H
E X T R Ā B V M N O (I N F R O N T O F) P
L B G N N T E S O Z U L E P I V O F M R
O K Q F S K O A W X X N Q A U K P R L A
W P O K Y A N C X D T D T X R P G X D E
N U R K K T T L O K Ā S D O J Z O X G T
Z Q Q O R H O L K N W I P H F H D B H E
L N R Q P E P W I F T A I C V P A S T R
O W F M X E O H A N Z R C P I L O T T K
A G S L J C F S W R F F Ā E R U G E O K
A W I T H F E B L X D R J R I M C T L R
G O S P D M H B J F Y U Ā L J L S Q A D
A D F F J H K T F H B I K O F U O O Q F
I Q P B S C L Y Y V B W J B J M U A G N
N A C R O S S U P E R W R A F C E B X U
S X X N P S W V M Y P H T J X H X K D W
T Q H O L O A K E S P O G O E K C E Z I
F G X R F H V W X U Z Q B B A L M U J B
O V E R A B O V E B E Y O N D T T E A D
```

It's In There!

That's right. Hidden in this jumble of letters are not only all of the Latin words that we are reviewing, but also the English translations. How many can you find?

ad - to, toward
ante - before
apud - with
circā - around
contrā - against
extrā - outside of
infrā - below
inter - between

intrā - within
iuxtā - near
ob - in front of
per - through
post - after
praeter - past
prope - near

propter - on account of
secundum - along
super - over, above, beyond
suprā - over, above, on top of
trāns - across
ultrā - beyond

Chapter 27

Nuts & Bolts

You know the drill. Pardon the pun.

ACROSS

3. I choose
4. hard (f)
7. high (f)
9. I ask
10. high (n)
12. I judged
16. bare (n)
17. worst (m)
18. bare (m)
19. smallest (f)
23. to judge
25. hard (m)
26. to ask
27. I go
28. hard (n)
29. I went
30. I give

DOWN

1. chosen
2. to give
3. I chose
5. asked
6. judged
8. given
10. high (m)
11. gone
13. to go
14. worst (n)
15. smallest (m)
16. bare (f)
20. I judge
21. to choose
22. worst (f)
24. I asked
28. I gave

Mountain biking, I go!

PLURAL

SINGULAR

īmus

is

ītis

ōe

sī

eunt

it

īmus

ītis

eō

is

īmus

ītis

it

eunt

eō

You're here at the bike shop with all of that Christmas, babysitting, and lawn-mowing cash you've earned. Can you figure out which spokes (circle them) go with each bike?
NOTE: Look carefully. One bike only takes singular forms, the other plural.

FREEZING COLD

What can warm up this frigid cold? These mixed-up words are all from this week's vocabulary. Can you unscramble them and find the hidden phrase? Use the hints if you need to.

GŌRO ⬜⬜⬜⬜ 12

XIIEMTERSĀ ⬜⬜⬜⬜⬜⬜⬜⬜⬜⬜⬜ 13

OĪGRVĀ ⬜⬜⬜⬜⬜⬜ 10

SMSIEAP ⬜⬜⬜⬜⬜⬜⬜ 2

TĀPROE ⬜⬜⬜⬜⬜⬜ 3

TTMPOĀU ⬜⬜⬜⬜⬜⬜⬜

MISVXĀĪETI ⬜⬜⬜⬜⬜⬜⬜⬜⬜⬜ 4

MDNUŪ ⬜⬜⬜⬜⬜

RŪUDS ⬜⬜⬜⬜⬜ 9

ĀTĪOPV ⬜⬜⬜⬜⬜⬜ 16

DVĪAŌN ⬜⬜⬜⬜⬜⬜

ŌE ⬜⬜

OĀGRER ⬜⬜⬜⬜⬜⬜ 15

TGUĀRMO ⬜⬜⬜⬜⬜⬜⬜

MAIMIN ⬜⬜⬜⬜⬜⬜ 6

ASLTU ⬜⬜⬜⬜⬜ 1

LAUMT ⬜⬜⬜⬜⬜ 14

UTŌNĀMD ⬜⬜⬜⬜⬜⬜⬜ 5

ŌDĀERN ⬜⬜⬜⬜⬜⬜ 7

IMMMUIN ⬜⬜⬜⬜⬜⬜⬜ 8

MSISMEUP ⬜⬜⬜⬜⬜⬜⬜⬜ 11

⬜⬜⬜⬜⬜ | w⬜⬜⬜⬜ | y⬜⬜⬜ | h⬜⬜⬜⬜!
1 2 3 4 5 — 6 7 8 9 — 10 11 12 — 13 14 15 16

Clues

I ask
to judge
I asked
worst
to choose
chosen
I judged
bare
hard
I chose
I gave
I go
to ask
asked
smallest
high
high
given
to give
smallest
worst

Chapter 28

Word Crossing

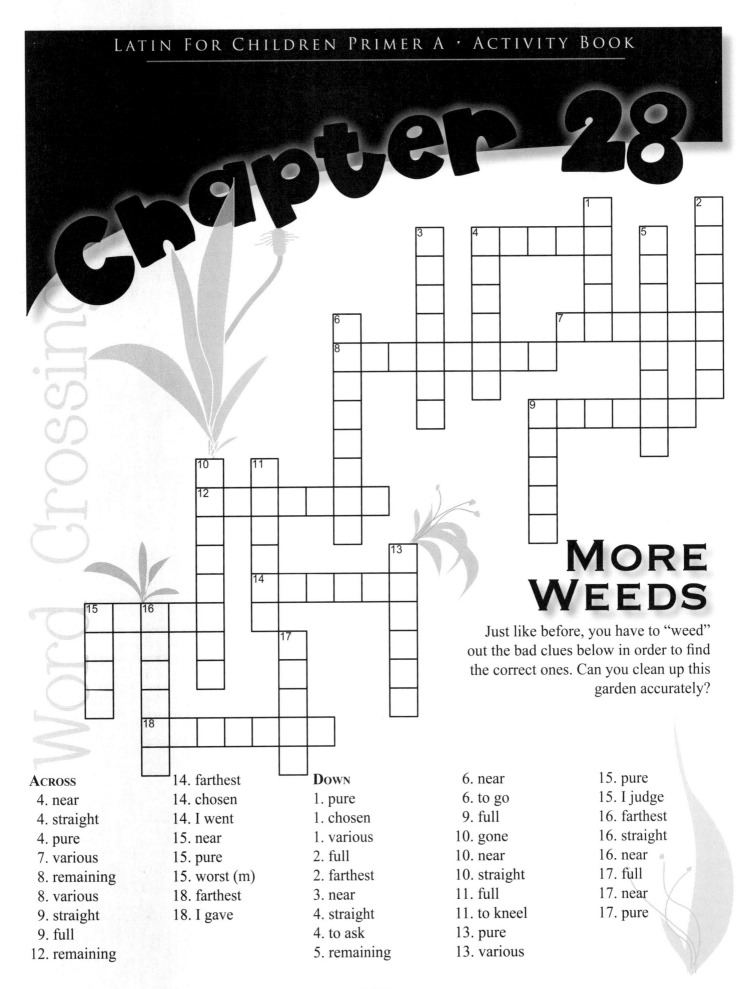

MORE WEEDS

Just like before, you have to "weed" out the bad clues below in order to find the correct ones. Can you clean up this garden accurately?

ACROSS
4. near
4. straight
4. pure
7. various
8. remaining
8. various
9. straight
9. full
12. remaining
14. farthest
14. chosen
14. I went
15. near
15. pure
15. worst (m)
18. farthest
18. I gave

DOWN
1. pure
1. chosen
1. various
2. full
2. farthest
3. near
4. straight
4. to ask
5. remaining
6. near
6. to go
9. full
10. gone
10. near
10. straight
11. full
11. to kneel
13. pure
13. various
15. pure
15. I judge
16. farthest
16. straight
16. near
17. full
17. near
17. pure

This puzzle/game is much like Bingo. Fill out the puzzle by circling the correct person, tense, and number for each Latin word in the gray box. When you get an entire row or column finished, scream out, "BINGO!" Just how many of these blocks can you fill out?

LATIN BINGO!

WE'VE DONE THIS ONE FOR YOU.

ībit

1st	2nd	3rd
Present	Future	Imperf.
Singular		Plural

(circled: 3rd, Future, Singular)

ībam

1st	2nd	3rd
Present	Future	Imperf.
Singular		Plural

eunt

1st	2nd	3rd
Present	Future	Imperf.
Singular		Plural

ībitis

1st	2nd	3rd
Present	Future	Imperf.
Singular		Plural

īs

1st	2nd	3rd
Present	Future	Imperf.
Singular		Plural

it

1st	2nd	3rd
Present	Future	Imperf.
Singular		Plural

ītis

1st	2nd	3rd
Present	Future	Imperf.
Singular		Plural

ībat

1st	2nd	3rd
Present	Future	Imperf.
Singular		Plural

ībātis

1st	2nd	3rd
Present	Future	Imperf.
Singular		Plural

ībō

1st	2nd	3rd
Present	Future	Imperf.
Singular		Plural

ībās

1st	2nd	3rd
Present	Future	Imperf.
Singular		Plural

ībis

1st	2nd	3rd
Present	Future	Imperf.
Singular		Plural

ībunt

1st	2nd	3rd
Present	Future	Imperf.
Singular		Plural

īmus

1st	2nd	3rd
Present	Future	Imperf.
Singular		Plural

ībant

1st	2nd	3rd
Present	Future	Imperf.
Singular		Plural

ībimus

1st	2nd	3rd
Present	Future	Imperf.
Singular		Plural

eō

1st	2nd	3rd
Present	Future	Imperf.
Singular		Plural

ībāmus

1st	2nd	3rd
Present	Future	Imperf.
Singular		Plural

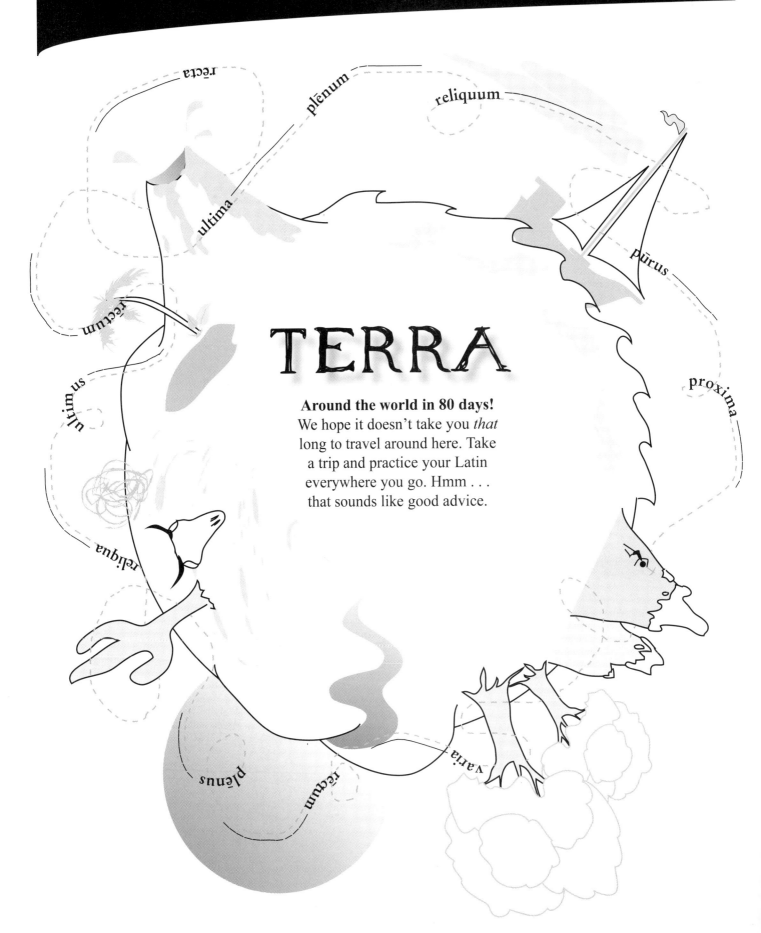

recta

plēnum

reliquum

ultima

pūrus

rectum

proxima

TERRA

Around the world in 80 days!
We hope it doesn't take you *that*
long to travel around here. Take
a trip and practice your Latin
everywhere you go. Hmm . . .
that sounds like good advice.

ultimus

reliqua

varia

plēnus

rēgnum

Chapter 29

The evil wizard captured the Latin words and had them locked up in his mazelike castle. A huge chunk of the wall has fallen down, allowing the Latin words to escape. Are you brave enough to work your way through the maze and help free the few remaining Latin words? Find them and translate below.

EW

RESCUE MISSION

plēnus   ultimum

dūrum

dōnātum

existimāvī

varium

dūrus   cōram

tenus   rēctum

pūrum   proxima

reliquum   ītum

existimō   dōnāvī

minimus   altus

spoon

cum

mirror

start

escape

bowl

apple

sine

fork

ex   rug

prae

Found:

_____, _____

_____, _____

_____, _____

_____, _____

Break In!

Can you help catch the international spies trying to break in?
If you can crack their code below, you'll save the day. HINT: This week's vocabulary.

code breaker

A	B	C	D	E	F	G	H	I	J	K	L	M	N	O	P	Q	R	S	T	U	V	W	X	Y	Z
						11											26		22	6	24	12			

$$\overset{\bar{\text{A}}\ \ \text{R}}{\underline{13\ 26}}\ ,\ \underline{1\ 23}\ ,\ \overset{\text{R}}{\underline{20\ 26\ 13\ 21}}\ ,\ \underline{23\ 4}\ \cdots\cdots$$

$$\overset{\text{R}}{\underline{5\ 13\ 26\ 1\ 21}}\ ,\ \underline{20\ 1\ 5\ 14}\overset{\text{-T}}{\underline{22\ 13}}\ \text{-}\underline{20\ 1\ 5\ 14}$$

$$\overset{\text{W}\ \ \text{T}}{\underline{12\ 25\ 22\ 2}}$$

$$\overset{\text{U}}{\underline{5\ 6\ 21}}\ ,\ \overset{\text{W}\ \ \text{T}}{\underline{12\ 25\ 22\ 2}}$$

$$\overset{\bar{\text{E}}}{\underline{9}}\ ,\ \overset{\text{W}}{\underline{9\ 13\ 12\ 15}}\ \overset{\text{R}}{\underline{20\ 26\ 13\ 21}}\ ,\ \overset{\text{R}}{\underline{20\ 26\ 13\ 21}}$$

$$\overset{\bar{\text{E}}\ \ \ \text{R}}{\underline{13\ 26\ 14\ 7}}\ ,\ \overset{\text{U}\ \ \text{T}}{\underline{13\ 6\ 22\ \ 13\ 20}}$$

$$\underline{25\ 15}\ +\ \overset{\text{T}\ \ \ \text{V}}{\underline{1\ 23\ 8\ 1\ 22\ 25\ 24\ 14}}\ ,\ \underline{25\ 15}$$

$$\underline{25\ 15}\ +\ \overset{\text{U}\ \ \ \ \text{T}\ \ \ \text{V}}{\underline{1\ 5\ 5\ 6\ 3\ 1\ 22\ 25\ 24\ 14}}\ ,\ \overset{\text{T}}{\underline{25\ 15\ 22\ 13}}$$

$$\overset{\text{R}}{\underline{10\ 26\ 1\ 14}}\ ,\ \underline{25\ 15}\ \overset{\text{R}\ \ \ \ \text{T}}{\underline{20\ 26\ 13\ 15\ 22\ \ 13\ 20}}$$

$$\overset{\text{R}\bar{\text{O}}}{\underline{10\ 26}}\ ,\ \overset{\text{R}}{\underline{23\ 14\ 20\ 13\ 26\ 14}}\ ,\ \underline{13\ 15}\ \underline{23\ 14\ 2\ 1\ 8\ 20}$$

$$\underline{13\ 20}$$

$$\underline{3\ 25\ 15\ 14}\ ,\ \overset{\text{W}\ \ \ \text{T}\ \ \ \ \ \text{U}\ \text{T}}{\underline{12\ 25\ 22\ 2\ \ 13\ 6\ 22}}$$

$$\overset{\text{U}}{\underline{3\ 6\ 23}}\ +\ \overset{\text{T}\ \ \ \text{V}}{\underline{1\ 23\ 8\ 1\ 22\ 25\ 24\ 14}}\ ,\ \overset{\text{U}\ \ \ \ \text{R}}{\underline{6\ 15\ 9\ 14\ 26}}$$

$$\overset{\text{U}}{\underline{3\ 6\ 23}}\ +\ \overset{\text{U}\ \ \ \ \text{T}\ \ \ \text{V}}{\underline{1\ 5\ 5\ 6\ 3\ 1\ 22\ 25\ 24\ 14}}\ ,\ \overset{\text{U}}{\underline{6\ 10}}$$

$$\overset{\text{T}}{\underline{22\ 13}}$$

$$\overset{\text{T}\ \ \ \ \ \text{U}}{\underline{22\ 14\ 15\ 6\ 3}}\ ,\ \overset{\text{T}\ \ \ \ \ \text{T}}{\underline{22\ 13\ \ 22\ 2\ 14}}\ \overset{\text{T}\ \ \ \ \ \ \text{T}}{\underline{14\ 7\ \ 22\ 14\ 15\ 22}}$$

$$\overset{\text{T}}{\underline{13\ 20}}\ ,\ \overset{\text{U}\ \ \ \ \text{T}}{\underline{6\ 10\ \ 22\ 13}}\ ,\ \overset{\text{W}\ \ \ \ \ \ \text{T}}{\underline{9\ 13\ 12\ 15\ \ 22\ 13}}\ ,\ \underline{1\ 3}$$

$$\overset{\text{R}}{\underline{20\ 1\ 26\ \ 1\ 3}}$$

Need a hint? Look on the top of the next page.

Tenus, anyone?

Can you draw a line and match the correct Latin with its English translation?
We've also mixed in a few words from previous weeks for practice.

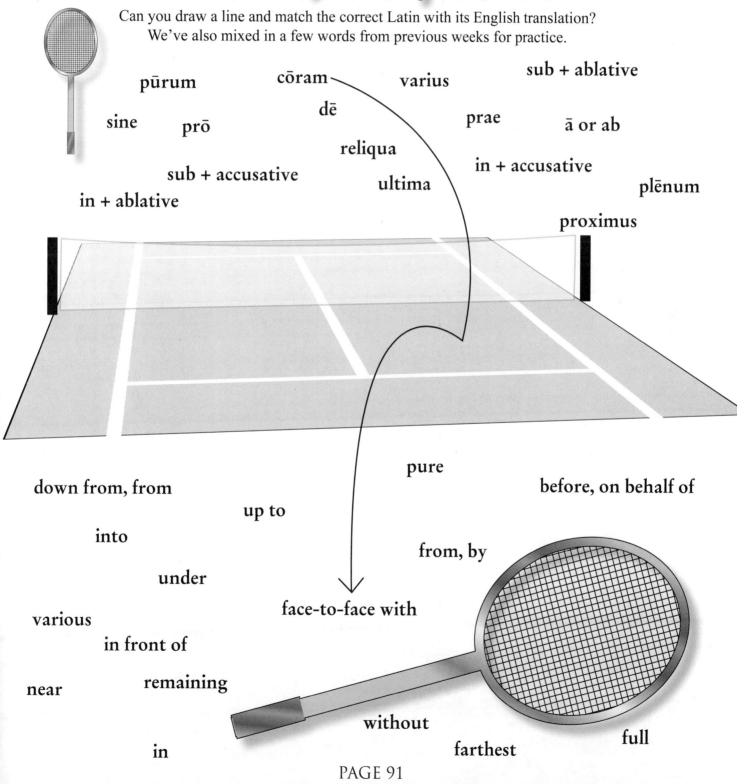

pūrum   cōram   varius   sub + ablative

sine   prō   dē   prae   ā or ab

        reliqua   in + accusative

sub + accusative   ultima   plēnum

in + ablative   proximus

down from, from   pure   before, on behalf of

        up to

into   from, by

        under

various   face-to-face with

    in front of

near   remaining

                without   full

        in   farthest

Chapter 30

sweet

Candy Man

Here's a sweet little puzzle just for you.

Jaw Breaker

ACROSS
4. I dine
6. to approach
9. sung
10. I sing
12. I am present
13. I went out
14. dined
15. I go away
16. to sing
20. gone out
21. remembered
23. to be present
25. absent
26. to dine
28. I was present
29. gone

DOWN
1. accused
2. I remember
3. to name
5. I approached
7. I accuse
8. I dined
9. to remember
11. named
15. to go away
17. I am absent
18. to go out
19. I accused
22. I was absent
23. approached
24. I go out
27. I approach

CHOO—CHOO!

This is one busy station! Can you link up the Latin engines (words) at the top of the page with their correct boxcars (circle them)? Make sure you don't jump tracks!

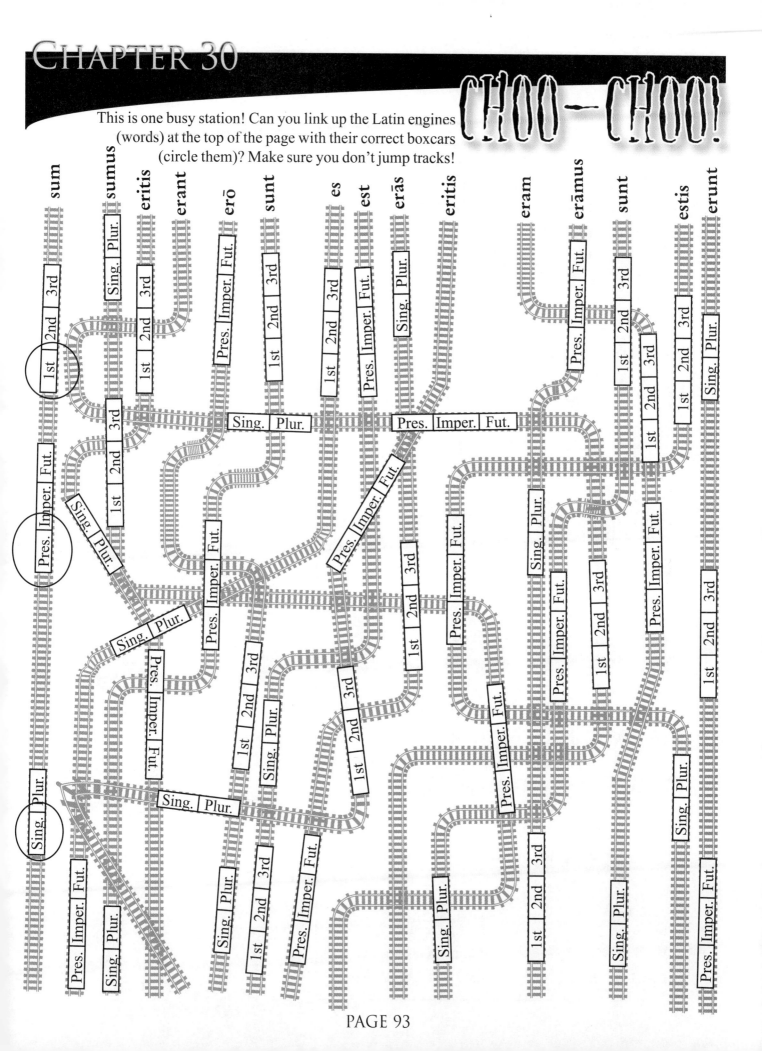

Translate, then find, following the sub from top to bottom.

SUB SEARCH

```
C Q W Z P P Y C T Z K Z D T A
S O Q U I U G U X M F Z R J P
C O M M E M O R Ā T U M Z L P
A V K M A P P E L L Ā T U M E
D B T U E F G Q X G S M V E L
Ī R Ī L L M Z Q A E A Y C S L
R X Q R Z C O D I K Ō Z S G Ā
E Z F I E W Ē R A B E Ō U D R
U B Y Y X G W N Ā V J O C V E
M B G R L J H C Ā R Y N L C S
A T C D V N L O I R E U J F S
A F U T Ū R U M A D E S S E Z
E P Z V J L C M M B V Y M T Y
X G P C A P P E L L Ā V Ī A Ā
I U H E A D M M N F C U Q B F
Ī Q A H L N A O R Ā J U R E U
N R O B K L T R M A T S D S Ī
A C C Ū S Ō Ō Ā E D X U J S J
Z C Ē N Ō U D V T S X C M E C
L W C L I E M Ī Y U S A H L O
B V B Ū A D F U Ī M M N C A M
H Q B W S D G G O L E T A C M
U D A D J Ā P S V A K Ā A C E
I I E D L V T B H E L R D Ū M
C W E C F I O U G R O E I S O
Ē H E S G U W R M W F H T Ā R
N Q F C A N T Ā V Ī L W U R Ō
Ā L P F A C C Ū S Ā V Ī M E A
V E X Ī R E A A R A D Ī Ī C D
Ī L Q E A H Y N B U H X A D E
T O D O H B W X T I M P P F Ō
I G I G T J I U O Ō Ī Z W C L
D I H J E H P T D Q K F S S Z
K R R T I K F F U E X I T U M
U Q W L Z X Y X Q M Y Y V M S
```

_____ - I am absent
_____ - to be absent
_____ - I was absent
_____ - absent
_____ - I am present
_____ - to be present
_____ - I was present
_____ - present
_____ - I go away
_____ - to go away
_____ - I went away
_____ - gone
_____ - I approach
_____ - to approach
_____ - I approached
_____ - approached
_____ - I go out
_____ - to go out
_____ - I went out
_____ - gone out
_____ - I dine
_____ - to dine
_____ - I dined
_____ - dined
_____ - I sing
_____ - to sing
_____ - I sang
_____ - sung
_____ - I name
_____ - to name
_____ - I named
_____ - named
_____ - I accuse
_____ - to accuse
_____ - I accused
_____ - accused
_____ - I remember
_____ - to remember
_____ - I remembered
_____ - remembered

REVIEW

Chapter 31

DIET PEAR CROSSWORD

Editor's Note:
What exactly is a "diet pear" crossword?

Designer's Note:
It's a zany twist on an old puzzle . . . with ½ the calories.

Editor's Note:
What?! How can a puzzle have ½ the calories?

Designer's Note:
Precisely!

Editor's Note:
But . . . but . . . My head hurts.

ACROSS			
2. *i Go*	23. _____	42. _____	16. _____
4. _____	24. _____		18. _____
6. _____	26. _____	**DOWN**	22. _____
7. _____	28. _____	1. _____	25. _____
8. _____	30. _____	2. _____	27. _____
9. _____	33. _____	3. _____	28. _____
10. _____	34. _____	5. _____	29. _____
12. _____	35. _____	7. _____	30. _____
17. _____	36. _____	9. _____	31. _____
19. _____	38. _____	11. _____	32. _____
20. _____	39. _____	13. _____	36. _____
21. _____	40. _____	14. _____	37. _____
	41. _____	15. _____	

Tread Marks

Derivatives are where the rubber hits the road. They're where you will find that Latin, often called a "dead language," is very much alive and well, influencing our modern-day English words. Learn your Latin vocabulary and you'll understand English words in a whole new way. Can you match the Latin tires with the correct tire marks by drawing lines between them?

Latin Tire

- varius
- dūrus
- ultimus
- plēnus
- pūrus
- rogō
- rēctus
- prō
- ā or ab
- ē or ex
- altus
- in + ablative
- sub + ablative
- absum
- minimus
- exeō
- optō
- accūsō
- commemorō

English Derivative Tread Marks

- opt, option, optional
- exit
- durable, endure
- accuse, accusation, accusatory
- interrogate, interrogatory
- exhale, exclude, expect
- rectify, rectangle, rectitude
- altitude, altimeter, alps
- submarine, submerge, subplot
- absent, absentee
- minimal, minimum, mini
- plenty, plenary
- pure, purify
- commemorate, commemorative, commemoration
- ultimate, ultimately, ultimatum
- various, variety, variable
- abnormal, abduct, abort
- inhale, include, inspect, import
- produce, proceed, progress

PACKED HOUSE

```
A D F U T Ū R U M A N Ē L P M
M U T I B A C Ō R A M U R Ū D
S U T L A R Ē C T A C I M Ō P
Ī V Ā R O M E M M O C I N R D
C A U Ō U M U L M U S Ō O I M
Ē D P D M R U M I S T X M I M
N R Ū P Ū I E T E Q I L N A N
Ā N Ā P E M T P Ā M U I A P C
T M E M O L N S U T M U A P E
U V R R I A L M I U N C M E X
M A Ā S D T L Ā S X C A M L I
Ō R S U Ō L S U R Ū E U C L S
E I Ū M N A N I S E T P Ē Ā T
B U C I Ā E U Ā X Ā K R N V I
A S C S T A T L L E Ā O Ā Ī M
C T A S U U M L T G D X V A Ā
O O O E M D E I O I Ē I Ī U T
P T M P M P Ū R S Ō M M V Q U
T U K M (P L Ē N U S) E U Ā I M
Ā S U A E X I T U M E S M L Ō
V T Ō R O M E M M O C P I E L
I V Ā N Ō D O O N M Ī M T R L
R O G Ā T U M R P V U O S D E
M U R Ū T U F Ā Ā T P C I Ū P
M U M I N I M S C T Ā P X R P
S S Ō R P I Ū Ē Ō L U T E U A
U U G N X C R U L T I M U S D
T R O O C M U N Ē L P C I M E
C Ū R A M U T O T A A M Ī D S
Ē P R O G Ā V Ī P N U I Ō R S
R E L I Q U U S T T Ī N R B E
U L T I M A C Ā I V Ā T N A C
M U I R A V R D Ī R A R Ū P V
A B E S S E A T E R Ā N Ē C N
```

Believe it or not, we pushed, we squeezed, we crammed all these words into one puzzle. How many can you find? If you run across a Latin word you don't know, look it up and practice it. You'll need it for what's to come!

rogō	pūrus	abitum
rogāre	pūra	adeō
rogāvī	pūrum	adīre
rogātum	rēctus	adiī
optō	rēcta	aditum
optāre	rēctum	exeō
optāvī	reliquus	exīre
optātum	reliqua	exiī
existimō	reliquum	exitum
existimāre	proximus	cēnō
existimāvī	proxima	cēnāre
existimātum	proximum	cēnāvī
dōnō	ultimus	cēnātum
dōnāre	ultima	cantō
dōnāvī	ultimum	cantāre
dōnātum	varius	cantāvī
eō	varia	cantātum
īre	varium	appellō
īvī	ab	appellāre
itum	cōram	appellāvī
altus	cum	appellātum
alta	dē	accūsō
altum	ex	accūsāre
dūrus	prae	accūsāvī
dūra	prō	accūsātum
dūrum	sine	commemorō
minimus	tenus	commemorāre
minima	absum	commemorāvī
minimum	abesse	commemorātum
nūdus	āfuī	
nūda	āfutūrum	
nūdum	adsum	
pessimus	adesse	
pessima	adfuī	
pessimum	adfutūrum	
~~plēnus~~	abeō	
plēna	abīre	
plēnum	abiī	

REVIEW

Chapter 32

Word Crossing

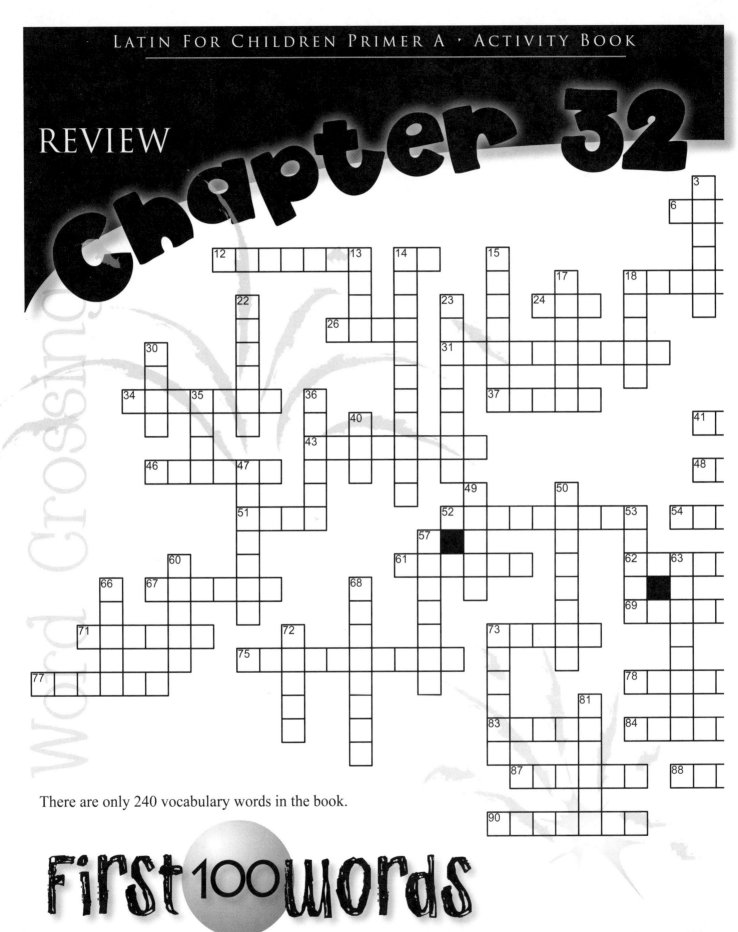

There are only 240 vocabulary words in the book.

First 100 words

The clues to this Latin crossword are found on page 100.

FIRST 100

ACROSS

4. road, way
6. ditch
10. water-carrier
11. friend (male)
12. maidservant
14. I give
18. public square
19. friend (female)
20. student/disciple (male)
24. I am
26. I prepare
27. turning point, goal
28. false
29. I fight
31. building
34. sister
37. table
38. sky
39. girl
41. wave
43. brother
44. I entrust
45. wolf
46. glory
48. servant (female)
51. I kill
52. danger
54. large, great
56. woman
61. fatherland
62. happy
64. known
67. ally
69. I look at
70. old
71. angry
73. gift
74. I point out
75. benefit, gift
77. I work

78. daughter
79. I wander
80. star
83. I delay
84. master (female)
85. I shout
87. I live
88. slave (female)
89. island
90. I explore
91. new

DOWN

1. true
2. school, game
3. garden
4. man
5. slave (male)
7. breeze
8. queen
9. servant (male)
10. I walk
13. water
14. I pointed out
15. town
16. teacher/master (male)
17. doubtful
18. fate
20. student (female)
21. I stand
22. page
23. reward
25. I love
28. story
30. boy
32. neck
33. I create
35. I change
36. I watch (or guard)
38. dinner
40. anger

42. master (male)
47. unknown
49. earth
50. help
53. bad
55. forest
56. window
57. joy
58. gate
59. I attack
60. good
63. example
65. calm (or bright or clear)
66. I tell
68. teacher (female)
72. I enter
73. I doubt
76. grain
81. I think
82. small
86. son

CHAPTER 32

You'll find the clues for this puzzle on page 103.

100 to 200

Across

2. on account of
4. I suffer
6. poet
8. along
11. near
12. river
14. I see
15. plan
17. sign
18. below
20. I order
22. through
26. earth, ground, land
27. against
28. sail
30. I remain
31. after
35. I increase
36. to, toward
37. before
38. rumor, report, fame
39. I grieve
40. silent
43. iron
45. year
46. blind
48. over, above, beyond
49. field
52. wall
53. silver
56. goddess
57. letter
59. rock
61. gold
64. god
65. at, by, near
66. hair
68. I blow
69. broad
70. roof
72. wall
73. I lie down
74. food for animals (fodder)
78. word
79. just
80. I estimate
81. enemy (personal)
83. over, above, on top of
84. within
86. I rejoice
87. level space, plain, field
89. farmer
90. I train
91. mind
92. wind

Down

1. grateful
3. leaf
5. long
7. horrendous
9. tired
10. benefit
13. around
16. near, next to
17. dirty
19. I hold
21. family
23. outside of
24. I call
25. I sail
28. I avoid
29. monument
30. I warn
32. in front of
33. cowardly
34. house
37. I plow
39. place
41. between, among
42. I have
44. horse
46. clear
47. heading, chapter
50. past
51. tomb
54. miserable
55. wild animal
58. I dare
60. settler
62. strange, wonderful
63. food
64. worthy
67. arm
71. conversation
75. silence
76. I guard against
77. across
80. dear
82. sailor
85. temple
88. prepared

CHAPTER 32

CATCH YOUR BREATH...

```
K L G W L
Z S S O N
D E Ī J D
Y B O F P
Q E I O A
```

Quick word search.
Can you find the one Latin
word and its translation
hidden here?

200 TO 240

Psst! The clues for this puzzle are on page 106. You're almost done!

LAST CROSSWORD BLITZ

LAST CROSSWORD BLITZ

ACROSS

2. out of
4. into
7. I remember
9. I dine
10. straight
12. I ask
14. I accuse
16. I approach
18. in
20. I name
22. high
23. across
25. I am present
26. from, by, away from
27. I judge
28. without
29. beyond
30. bare
33. worst
35. to the extent of
36. I give
37. near
38. up to

DOWN

1. down from, concerning, about
3. remaining
5. with
6. in front of
7. I sing
8. I go out
11. under
13. face-to-face with
14. I go away
15. I remembered
16. I am absent
17. full
19. farthest
21. pure
24. various
27. I go
31. hard
32. I choose
33. before, on behalf of
34. small

THAT'S ALL, FOLKS!

Thanks for playing!

CHAPTER 1

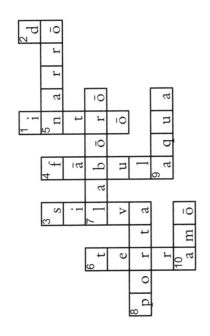

	Singular	Plural
1st person	amō	amāmus
2nd person	amās	amātis
3rd person	amat	amant

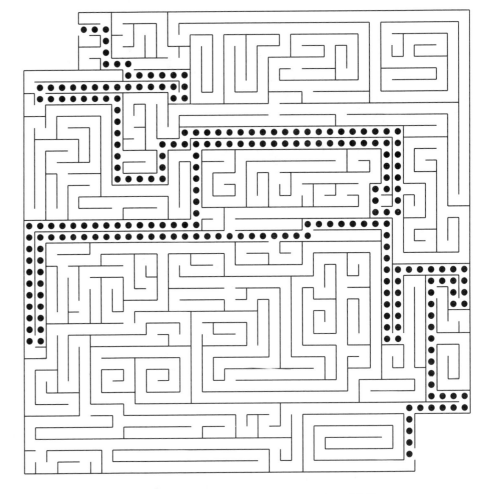

```
T M K B X L J Y L U S
B E W M D T H P Y V R
V Q R A L R U O R N M
I J L R V J Q R C B K
F I O K A Y B T V Q Q
I N T R Ō A D A E D Y
G B M G L Q E Ō M N C
U M N B U U C K O C Z
S B E Z W A R H X N N
A U I N G Z E S P O R
L A M Ō F J G F G R E
I A B Q G F C M X B P
L R B A L I F A V N D
W L S Ō J L Z L B W L
N H E X R U S I L V A
L A B M Y Ō A L H A Q
C K R G K W D A H Z Z
N B Q R W K G R C S I
N U K S Ō C X R I A X
Z G F D N O T I O S P
```

BONUS ANSWER:
fābula

MAZE ANSWERS:

intrātum - entered

narrō - I tell

labōrō - I work

LEAP FROG

**In <u>principiō</u> erat
<u>Verbum</u>.**
*(In the beginning was
the Word. —Latin
Vulgate)*

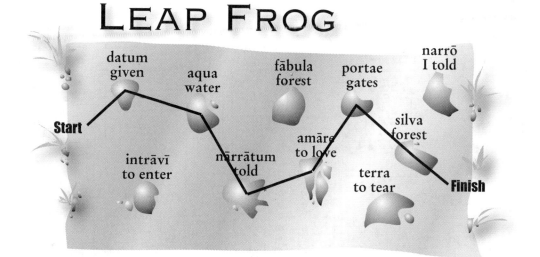

CHAPTER 2

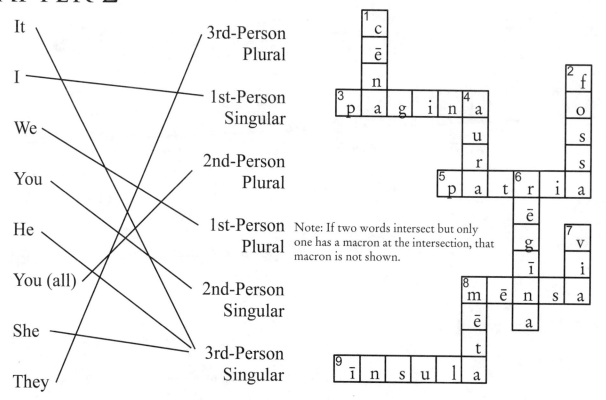

Note: If two words intersect but only
one has a macron at the intersection, that
macron is not shown.

	Singular	Plural
1st person	-ō	-mus
2nd person	-s	-tis
3rd person	-t	-nt

ENGLISH MAZE   LATIN MAZE

goal = **mēta, mētae**

fatherland = **pātria, pātriae**

queen = **rēgīna, rēgīnae**

pāgina = page

cēna = dinner

aura = breeze

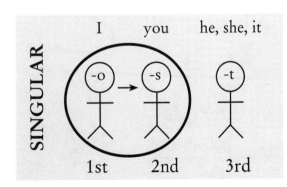
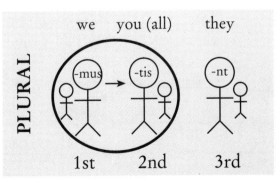

CHAPTER 3

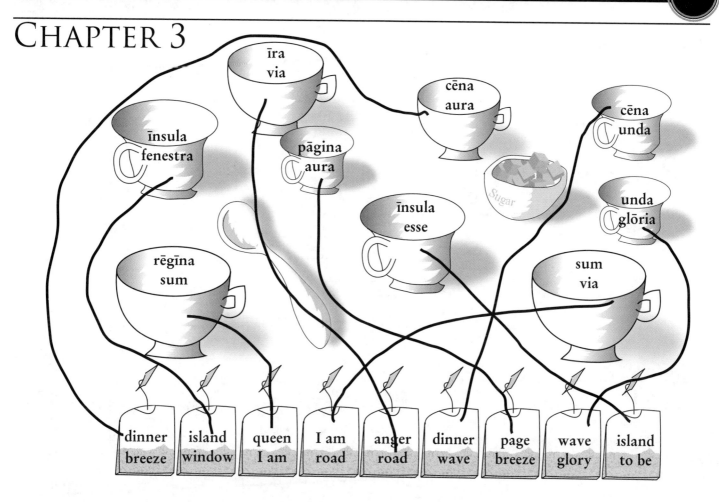

Arma virumque canō.
(Of arms and the man I sing. —Vergil's Aeneid)

Case	Noun Job	Singular	Plural
Nominative	SN, PrN	**mēnsa:** table	**mēnsae:** tables
Genitive	PNA	**mēnsae:** of the table	**mēnsārum:** of the tables
Dative	IO	**mēnsae:** to/for the table	**mēnsīs:** to/for the tables
Accusative	DO, OP	**mēnsam:** the table	**mēnsās:** the tables
Ablative	OP	**mēnsā:** by/with/from the table	**mēnsīs:** by/with/from the tables

SN = Subject Noun

PrN = Predicate Nominative

PNA = Possessive Noun

IO = Indirect Object

DO = Direct Object

OP = Object of the Preposition

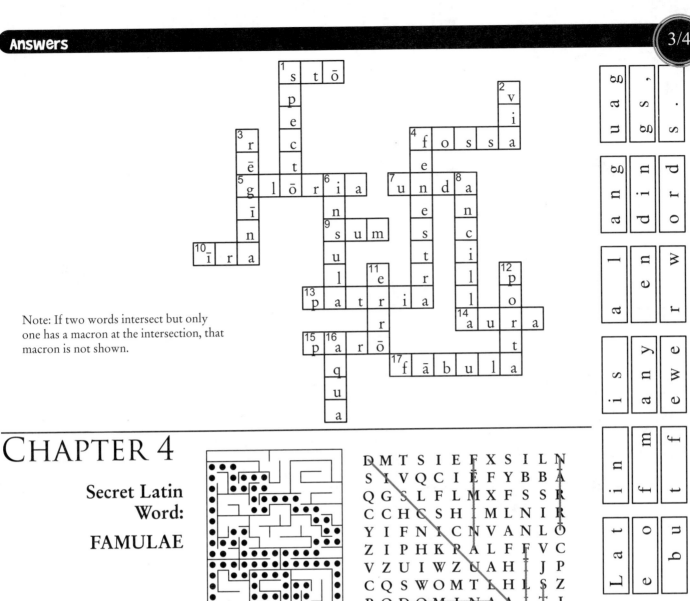

Note: If two words intersect but only one has a macron at the intersection, that macron is not shown.

CHAPTER 4

Secret Latin Word:

FAMULAE

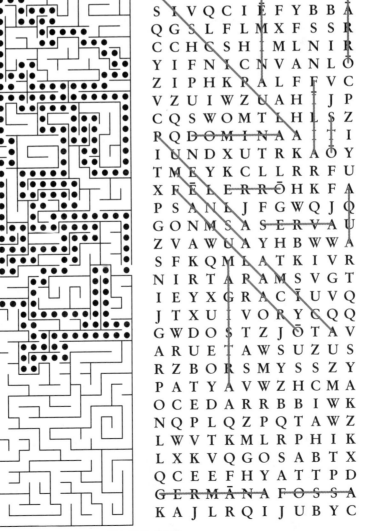

	Plural	Singular
Nominative	-ae	-a
Genitive	-ārum	-ae
Dative	-īs	-ae
Accusative	-ās	-am
Ablative	-īs	-ā

NOTE: Because of the reoccurrence of similar endings, the connecting lines can be drawn several ways. The above chart displays the correct connections.

LUEPAL, GLRI
PUELLA, GIRL
        10

MDNIAO, AMFELE MESATR
DOMINA, FEMALE MASTER
      2   13

AISTMGAR, AFEEML HCTAERE
MAGISTRA, FEMALE TEACHER
     1

MĀNARGE, ITRSES
GERMĀNA, SISTER
              4

LCPIUSIAD, EALFEM TDTSEUN
DISCIPULA, FEMALE STUDENT
        5   12   15

LAMUFA, FMEALE ENTVASR
FAMULA, FEMALE SERVANT
                  6   9

AREVS, EAEFML ELVAS
SERVA, FEMALE SLAVE
             11

IĒFANM, NAWMO
FĒMINA, WOMAN
              7

ĪMACA, EAMLEF DEFINR
AMĪCA, FEMALE FRIEND
    14   3

FIALĪ, DUEAHTGR
FILĪA, DAUGHTER
     8

I'M LEARNING LATIN!
1 2 3 4 5 6 7 8 9 10 11 12 13 14 15

CHAPTER 5

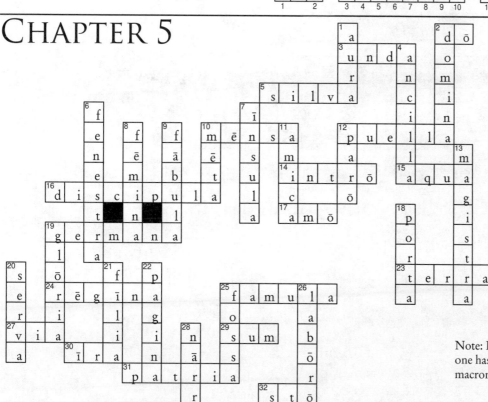

Note: If two words intersect but only one has a macron at the intersection, that macron is not shown.

...ated that an (error) ...as occured in the ...blishing of the article. The (family) of blue (aquatic) dol- ...phins was not what ...as giving off a ...onderful (aroma) on ...e BBQ it was the ...he tuna steaks that ...ent off the smell. ■

...e only (portable) ...sh in the tank. You ...n move it upstairs ...t it won't help the ...ld problem. ...t it free, (fabulous) ...d all in one easy ...yment. No money ...wn. We're here to ...our best & (serve) ...n the only (way) ...t we know. Yes, ...e rambling on and ...but I've got to ...me up with more ...l more text just to ...l the sp... More- ...there a... ...re us ...fill in ...

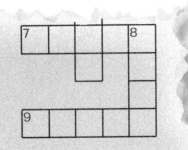

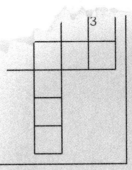

CUTES BABY AWAR...

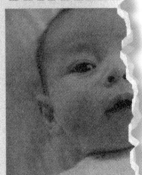

This year's a... winner was an... pick. The (female)... picked a (family)... such a cute chil... thought it migl... crime.

Not to domi... competition a... child, who w... cute as well, w... brought into... ning.

(Irritating) the sk... fair amount of... powder was... throughout the c... tition ar...

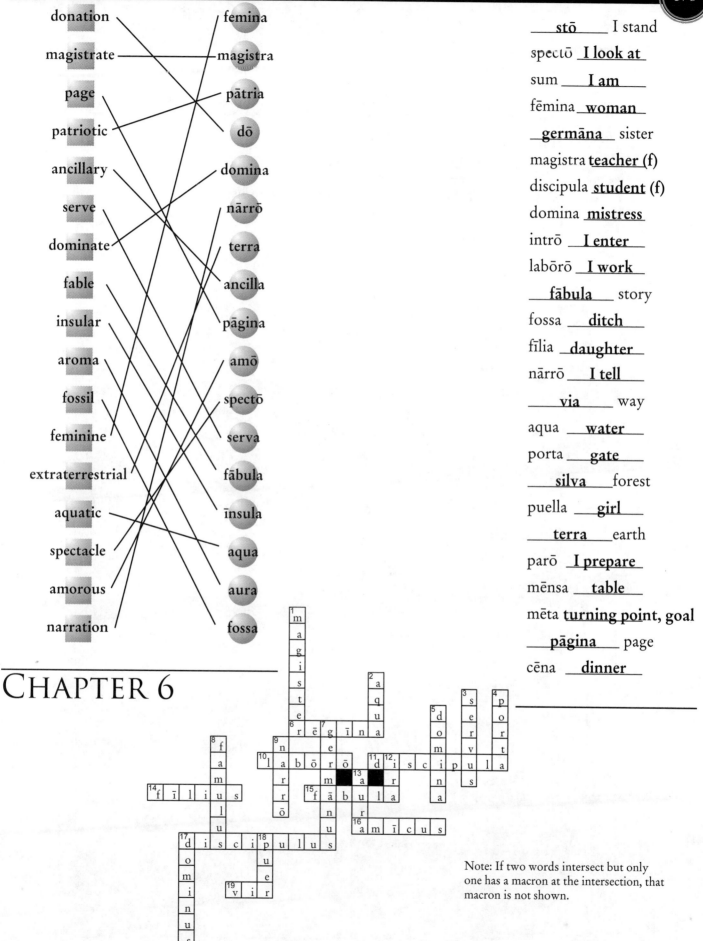

donation
magistrate
page
patriotic
ancillary
serve
dominate
fable
insular
aroma
fossil
feminine
extraterrestrial
aquatic
spectacle
amorous
narration

femina
magistra
pātria
dō
domina
nārrō
terra
ancilla
pāgina
amō
spectō
serva
fābula
īnsula
aqua
aura
fossa

__stō__ I stand
spectō __I look at__
sum __I am__
fēmina __woman__
__germāna__ sister
magistra __teacher (f)__
discipula __student (f)__
domina __mistress__
intrō __I enter__
labōrō __I work__
__fābula__ story
fossa __ditch__
fīlia __daughter__
nārrō __I tell__
__via__ way
aqua __water__
porta __gate__
__silva__ forest
puella __girl__
__terra__ earth
parō __I prepare__
mēnsa __table__
mēta __turning point__, goal
__pāgina__ page
cēna __dinner__

CHAPTER 6

Crossword:
1 m magister
2 aqua
6 rēgīna
10 labōrō
11 discipula
14 fīlius
15 fābula
16 amīcus
17 discipulus
19 vir
3 serva
4 porta
5 domina
8 fama
9 nerrō
13 a
18 puer

Note: If two words intersect but only one has a macron at the intersection, that macron is not shown.

PAGE 115

Case	Noun Job	Singular	Plural
Nominative	SN, PrN	**lūdus:** school	**lūdī:** schools
Genitive	PNA	**lūdī:** of the school	**lūdōrum:** of the schools
Dative	IO	**lūdō:** to/for the school	**lūdīs:** to/for the schools
Accusative	DO, OP	**lūdum:** the school	**lūdōs:** the schools
Ablative	OP	**lūdō:** by/with/from the school	**lūdīs:** by/with/from the schools

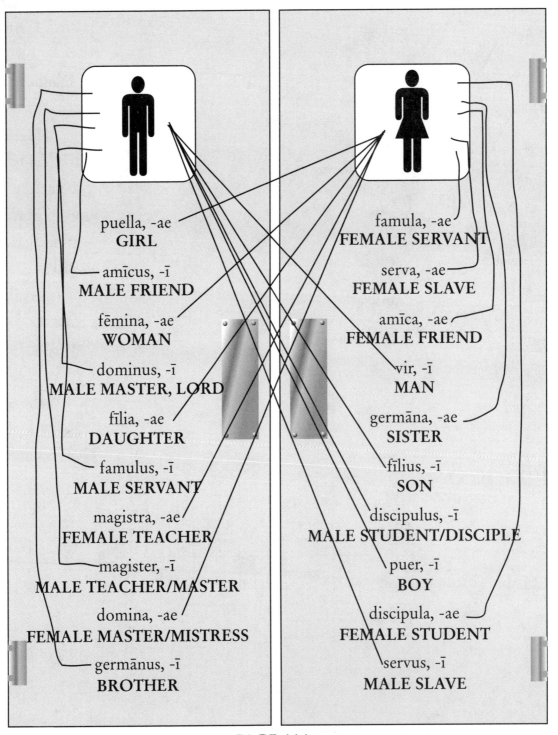

puella, -ae
GIRL

amīcus, -ī
MALE FRIEND

fēmina, -ae
WOMAN

dominus, -ī
MALE MASTER, LORD

fīlia, -ae
DAUGHTER

famulus, -ī
MALE SERVANT

magistra, -ae
FEMALE TEACHER

magister, -ī
MALE TEACHER/MASTER

domina, -ae
FEMALE MASTER/MISTRESS

germānus, -ī
BROTHER

famula, -ae
FEMALE SERVANT

serva, -ae
FEMALE SLAVE

amīca, -ae
FEMALE FRIEND

vir, -ī
MAN

germāna, -ae
SISTER

fīlius, -ī
SON

discipulus, -ī
MALE STUDENT/DISCIPLE

puer, -ī
BOY

discipula, -ae
FEMALE STUDENT

servus, -ī
MALE SLAVE

UDONSMI	D O M I N U S
IRV	V I R
UACSĪM	A M Ī C U S
EMSAIRTG	M A G I S T E R
UMGSEĀRN	G E R M Ā N U S
SLĪFUI	F Ī L I U S
UPILCUSDSI	D I S C I P U L U S
EPUR	P U E R
LASUFMU	F A M U L U S
RVSESU	S E R V U S

W E L L   D O N E

Cum tacent, clāmant.
(When they are silent, they shout. —Cicero)

CHAPTER 7

LATIN	ENGLISH
vigilō, vigilāre, vigilāvī , vigilātum	I watch (or guard), to watch, I watched, watched
clāmō, clāmāre, clāmāvī , clāmātum	I shout, to shout, I shouted, shouted
tardō, tardāre, tardāvī , tardātum	I delay, to delay, I delayed, delayed
habitō, habitāre, habitāvī , habitātum	I live, to live, I lived, lived
dēmōnstrō, dēmōnstrāre, dēmōnstrāvī , dēmōnstrātum	I point out, to point out, I pointed out, pointed out
lūdus, -ī	school, game
hortus, -ī	garden
lupus, -ī	wolf
socius, -ī	ally, associate
aquārius, -ī	water-carrier

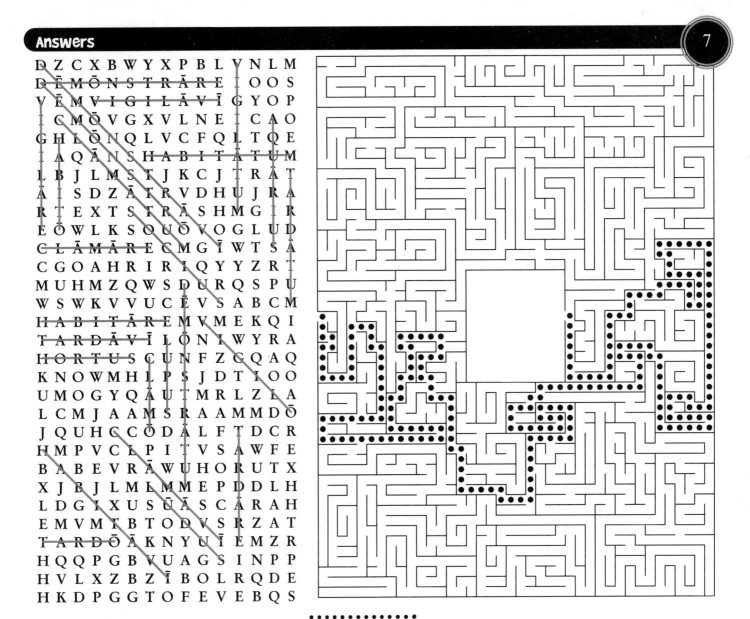

```
D Z C X B W Y X P B L V N L M
D Ē M Ō N S T R Ā R E I O O S
V Ē M V I G I L Ā V Ī G Y O P
I C M Ō V G X V L N E I C A O
G H L Ō N Q L V C F Q L T Q E
I A Q Ā N S H A B I T Ā T U M
L B J L M S T J K C J T R Ā T
Ā I S D Z Ā T R V D H U J R A
R T E X T S T R Ā S H M G I R
E Ō W L K S Q U Ō V O G L U D
C L Ā M Ā R E C M G Ī W T S Ā
C G O A H R I R I Q Y Y Z R T
M U H M Z Q W S D U R Q S P U
W S W K V V U C Ē V S A B C M
H A B I T Ā R E M V M E K Q I
T A R D Ā V Ī L Ō N I W Y R A
H O R T U S C U N F Z G Q A Q
K N O W M H L P S J D T I O O
U M O G Y Q Ā U T M R L Z I A
L C M J A A M S R A A M M D Ō
J Q U H C C Ō D Ā L F T D C R
H M P V C L P I T V S A W F E
B A B E V R Ā W U H O R U T X
X J B J L M L M M E P D D L H
L D G I X U S Ū Ā S C A R A H
E M V M T B T O D V S R Z A T
T A R D Ō Ā K N Y U I E M Z R
H Q Q P G B V U A G S I N P P
H V L X Z B Z I B O L R Q D E
H K D P G G T O F E V E B Q S
```

CARNIVAL SHOOT OUT!

NOTE: There are several ways to connect the pieces of this game. Use the charts below as reference.

WORDS FOUND (translated):

school - **lūdus**
wolf - **lupus**
to live - **habitāre**
shouted - **clāmātum**
I watched - **vigilāvī**
ally - **socius**

	Singular	Plural
Nominative	-us	-ī
Genitive	-ī	-ōrum
Dative	-ō	-īs
Accusative	-um	-ōs
Ablative	-ō	-īs

	Singular	Plural
1st person	sum (I am)	sumus (we are)
2nd person	es (you are)	estis (you all are)
3rd person	est (he, she, it is)	sunt (they are)

CHAPTER 8

ŌDUNM   D Ō N U M (1)

NOGPUŌP   O P P U G N Ō (8)

IXMILUAU   A U X I L I U M (2)

DANŌM   M A N D Ō (4)

ŌALBUM   A M B U L Ō (10)

IIEUIDFAMC   A E D I F I C I U M (3)

ULMACE   C A E L U M (5)

PGUNŌ   P U G N Ō (9)

EPUEMLXM   E X E M P L U M (6)

ŌNEC   N E C Ō (7)

D I V I D E   E T   R E G N A
1 2 3 4 5   6   7 8 9 10

For all neuter nouns, the <u>nominative</u> and <u>accusative</u> case forms are exactly the same.

Begin listing all the exceptions to the neuter rule below:

NONE!!

Case	Singular		Plural	
Nominative	**dōnum:** gift		**dōna:** gifts	
Genitive	**dōnī:** of the gift		**dōnōrum:** of the gifts	
Dative	**dōnō:** to/for the gift		**dōnīs:** to/for the gifts	
Accusative	**dōnum:** the gift		**dōna:** the gifts	
Ablative	**dōnō:** by/with/from the gift		**dōnīs:** by/with/from the gifts	

Crossword solution:

1 Across: necāre
3 Across: ambulāre
5 Across: oppugnātum
8 Across: pugnāvī
9 Across: ambulō
11 Across: mandāre
16 Across: necāvī
17 Across: mandō
18 Across: ambulāvī
19 Across: caelum
20 Across: mandātum

Down clues:
1 Down: necātum
2 Down: ambulum
4 Down: a... (auxilium)
5 Down: oppugnāvī
6 Down: pugnōum
7 Down: oppugnum
9 Down: aedificium
10 Down: maua
12 Down: ...arede
13 Down: nec
14 Down: dō
15 Down: pugnātum

Across

1. to kill
3. to walk
5. attacked
8. I fought
9. I walk
11. to entrust
16. I killed
17. I entrust
18. I walked
19. sky
20. entrusted

Down

1. killed
2. walked
4. help
5. I attacked
6. I fight
7. to attack
9. building
10. I enstrusted
12. example
13. I kill
14. gift
15. fought

MISSIN G!

CHAPTER 9

```
F D T U B N N V G G L H H U F E H X H L F V T I F M T M P E
L R G M E P A C R I A H G I O E V P O X Ū R L Q K A X B R C
C S C U N W B N O V V U O M R U E R N L U D Ū K W N T A A S
C M F P E R Ī C U L U M D H U I N Z G P F R U M F D X U E Z
S K S R F R P B F Q H T G I M M D D T E R R A S E Ö A D M Y
T K I J P W B B F G X A Y U N T D A B U C X W L N J V I G
E P V F C Q L F Q V V C S L J M U J R O U X X O S L T L U Z
W D F B I M X I B W S E T Y H O J D K L R W R M B J M U M Q
I P W I U O P P I D U M R C O L L U M S E E O W L K B C M X
C Y R U M O H T D X K F U R X W U K Q D R D T H B L N D H T
S I W W E Y B I C J K P M G C Z C O C G M Z L U L N W W O O
X J I O E C T R V E C Ē N A T C H T I D L W J W S W J D P R
```

LATIN	ENGLISH
fātum, -ī	fate
forum, -ī	public square
oppidum, -ī	town
perīculum, -ī	danger
frūmentum, -ī	grain
praemium, -ī	reward
astrum, -ī	star
beneficium, -ī	benefit, gift
gaudium, -ī	joy
collum, -ī	neck

In Latin, you can usually tell what the subject of a sentence is because it is in the <u>nominative</u> case.

Extra Words Found: mandō, lūdus, unda, cēna

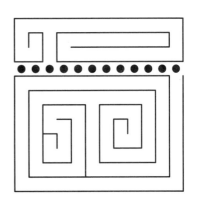

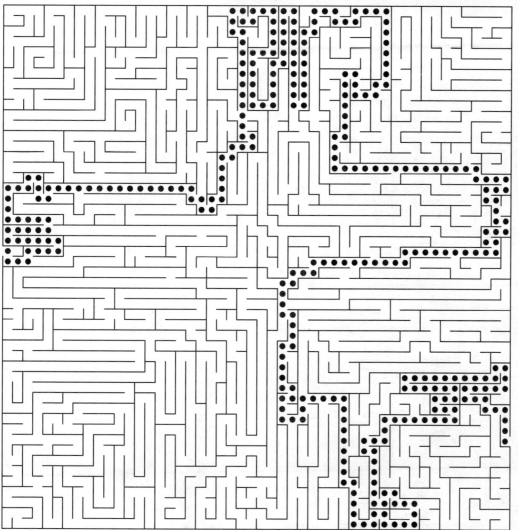

BRIDGE:
fātum - fate
forum - public square
oppidum - town
perīculum - danger
frūmentum - grain
praemium - reward
astrum - star
beneficium - benefit, gift
gaudium - joy
collum - neck

**SECRET
MAZE WORD:**
astrum - star

Case	Noun Job	Singular	Plural
Nominative	subject (SN), predicate nominative (PrN)	**-um**	**-a**
Genitive	possessive noun (PNA)	**-ī**	**-ōrum**
Dative	indirect object (IO)	**-ō**	**-īs**
Accusative	direct object (DO), object of the preposition (OP)	**-um**	**-a**
Ablative	object of the preposition (OP)	**-ō**	**-īs**

CHAPTER 10

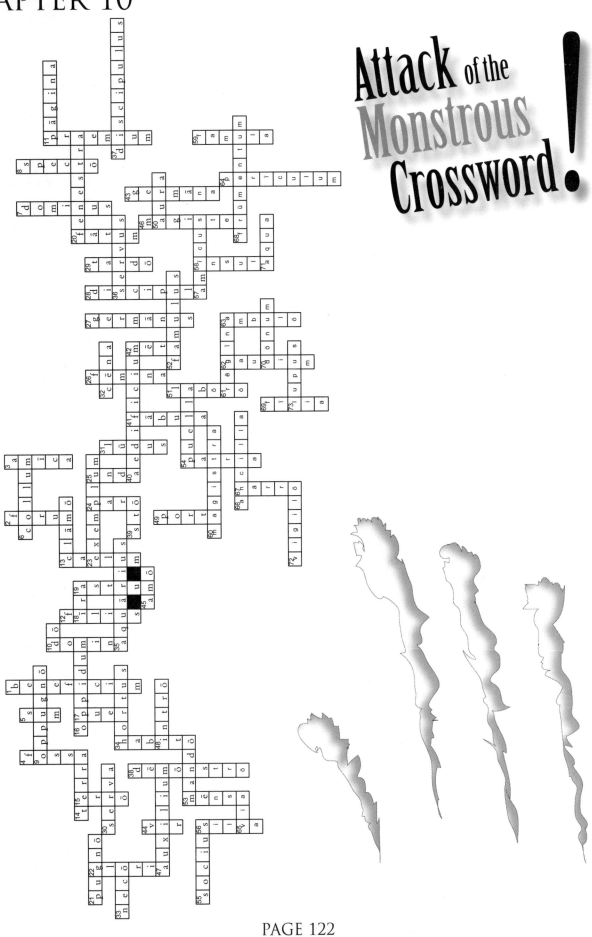

Attack of the Monstrous Crossword!

CHAPTER 11

creō - I create	**cōgitāre** - to think	**dubitāvī** - I doubted	**vēra** - true
creāre - to create	**cōgitāvī** - I thought	**dubitātum** - doubted	**vērum** - true
creāvī - I created	**cōgitātum** - thought	**magnus** - large, great	**falsus** - false
creātum - created	**mūtō** - I change	**magna** - large, great	**falsa** - false
explōrō - I explore	**mūtāre** - to change	**magnum** - large, great	**falsum** - false
explōrāre - to explore	**mūtāvī** - I changed	**parvus** - small	**dubius** - doubtful
explōrāvī - I explored	**mūtātum** - changed	**parva** - small	**dubia** - doubtful
explōrātum - explored	**dubitō** - I doubt	**parvum** - small	**dubium** - doubtful
cōgitō - I think	**dubitāre** - to doubt	**vērus** - true	

Menu

-us	Singular	Nom.	Masculine
-ārum	Plural	Gen.	Feminine
-ōs	Plural	Acc.	Masculine
-um	Singular	Nom.	Neuter
-a	Plural	Acc.	Neuter
-ō	Singular	Dat.	Neuter
-īs	Plural	Dat.	Feminine

Cōgitō ergo sum.
(I *think* therefore I *am*. —Descartes)

Laundry

magnus, m., large, great
magna, f., large, great
magnum, n., large, great
parvus, m., small
parva, f., small
parvum, n., small
vērus, m., true
vēra, f., true

vērum, n., true
falsus, m., false
falsa, f., false
falsum, n., false
dubius, m., doubtful
dubia, f., doubtful
dubium, n., doubtful

CHAPTER 12

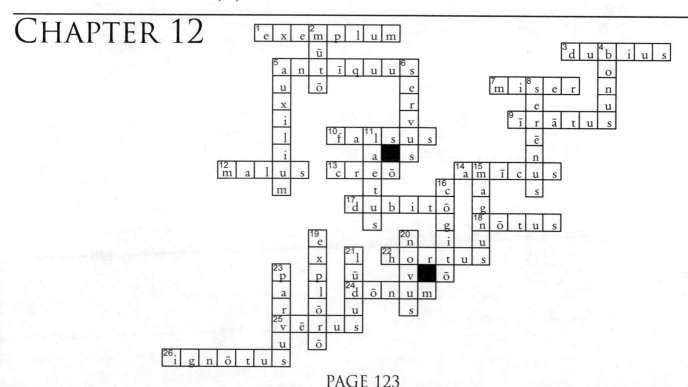

	Singular			Plural		
	Masculine	Feminine	Neuter	Masculine	Feminine	Neuter
Nominative (PA)	magnus	magna	magnum	magnī	magnae	magna
Genitive	magnī	magnae	magnī	magnōrum	(magnārum)	(magnōrum)
Dative	magnō	(magnae)	magnō	magnīs	magnīs	magnīs
Accusative (OCA)	magnum	(magnam)	magnum	(magnōs)	(magnās)	magna
Ablative	magnō	magnā	(magnō)	(magnīs)	(magnīs)	magnīs

```
b o n u s ,    g o o d    ( m )
  b o n a ,    g o o d    ( f )
b o n u m ,    g o o d    ( n )
  m a l u s ,    b a d    ( m )
  m a l u m ,    b a d    ( n )
  n ō t u s ,  k n o w n    ( m )
  n ō t a ,    k n o w n  ( f )
  n ō t u m ,  k n o w n    ( n )
  n o v u m ,    n e w    ( n )
a n t ī q u u s ,    o l d    ( m )
  a n t ī q u a ,    o l d    ( f )
  a n t ī q u u m ,    o l d    ( n )
  ī r ā t u s ,    a n g r y    ( m )
  l a e t u m ,    h a p p y    ( n )
m i s e r ,      m i s e r a b l e    ( m )
m i s e r a ,  m i s e r a b l e    ( f )
m i s e r u m ,  m i s e r a b l e    ( n )
```

Cōgitō ergo sum.

(I think therefore I am. —Descartes)

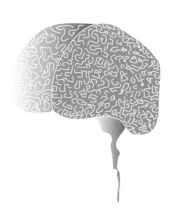

CHAPTER 13

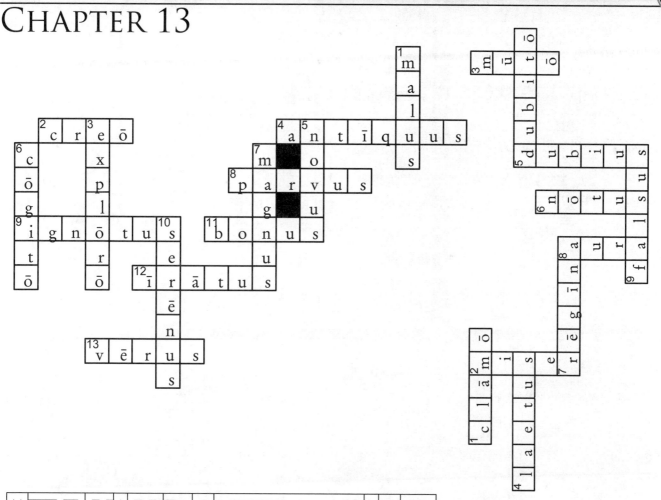

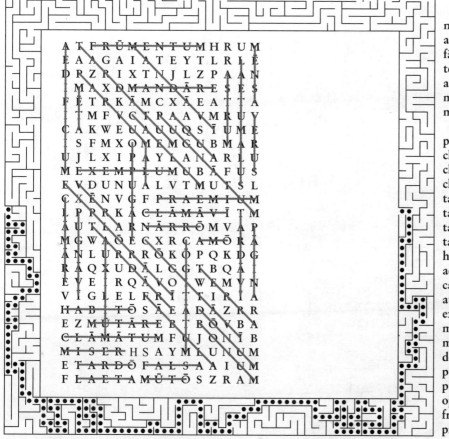

nārrō – I tell
aqua – water
fābula – story
terra – earth
amō – I love
mēnsa – table
mēta – turning point,
          goal
pāgina – page
clāmāre – to shout
clāmāvī – I shouted
clāmātum – shouted
tardō – I delay
tardāre – to delay
tardāvī – I delayed
tardātum – delayed
habitō – I live
aedificium – building
caelum – sky
auxilium – help
exemplum – example
mandāre – to entrust
mandāvī – I entrusted
dōnum – gift
pugnāvī – I fought
pugnātum – fought
oppugnāre – to attack
frūmentum – grain
praemium – reward

astrum – star
explōrāvī – I explored
cōgitāvī – I thought
cōgitātum – thought
mūtō – I change
mūtāre – to change
parvum – small
vērus – true
vēra – true
falsa – false
bonum – good (n)
malus – bad (m)
mala – bad (f)
laeta – happy (f)
laetum – happy (n)
miserus – miserable (m)

Spy Games!

APULEL	P U E L L A		

APULEL — P U E L L A (6, 10)
MFIAĒN — F Ē M I N A (1)
LFAĪI — F Ī L I A (4)
MNRGĀAE — G E R M Ā N A (3)
MAGATRSI — M A G I S T R A (7)
LDSIAPICU — D I S C I P U L A (9)
NIOAMD — D O M I N A
AMULFA — F A M U L A (5)
VSEAR — S E R V A (2)
ACMAĪ — A M Ī C A (8)

F E M A L E S   A L L
(1 2 3 4 5 6 7   8 9 10)

IRV — V I R
MNĀRSGEU — G E R M Ā N U S (7, 6)
UUAFSLM — F A M U L U S (8)
GATSMIER — M A G I S T E R (2)
LUIUPDCSIS — D I S C I P U L U S (9, 5)
IONUDSM — D O M I N U S (11, 4, 3)
URPE — P U E R
VERSSU — S E R V U S
SUĪCMA — A M Ī C U S (1)
LUIFĪS — F Ī L I U S (10)

M E N ,   y O U N G   A N D   O L D
(1 2 3   4 5 6 7   8 6 9   4 10 11)

CHAPTER 14

ACROSS
2. farmer
7. settler
11. of the field
12. I increase
13. I have
16. I held
17. to hold
18. of the poet
21. to have
22. sailor
24. I saw
27. increased
28. to order
29. to see
30. ordered

DOWN
1. I increased
3. I order
4. to increase
5. I see
6. I ordered
8. of the farmer
9. poet
10. of the sailor
14. field
15. of the settler
19. I hold
20. I had
23. seen
25. had
26. held

PYRAMID CLIMB
ager - field
augeō - I increase
vīsum - seen

	Singular	Plural
1st person	**videō**	**vidēmus**
2nd person	**vidēs**	**vidētis**
3rd person	**videt**	**vident**

videō, vidēre, vīdī, vīsum = I see, to see, I saw, seen

CHAPTER 15

Ingredients

animus - mind
animī - of the mind
campus - level space, plain, field
campusī - of the level space, plain, field
annus - year
annī - of the year
mūrus - wall
mūrī - of the wall
cibus - food
cibī - of the food
ventus - wind
ventī - of the wind
equus - horse
equī - of the horse
ferus - wild animal
ferī - of the wild animal
fluvius - river
fluviī - of the river

PATERN A
Subject noun
Simple form
Verb
SN
V
PatA

PATTERN B
Linking verb
Pattern of "B"eing
PatB
2 nouns
LV
SN
PRN
Predicate nominative

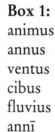

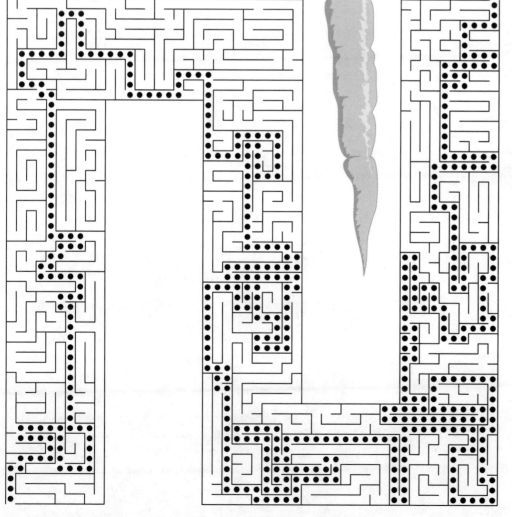

Box 1:
animus
annus
ventus
cibus
fluvius
annī

Box 2:
food
campus
mūrus
fluvius
mind
ventus

Box 3:
of the level space, plain,
    field
of the wild animal
walls
of the horse
campus

CHAPTER 16

Note: If two words intersect but only one has a macron at the intersection, that macron is not shown.

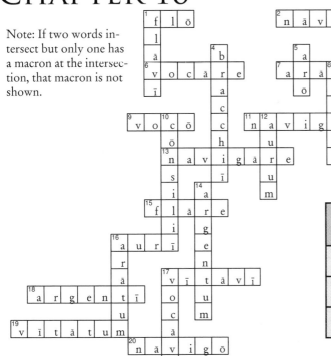

Ars longa, **vita** brevis.
(_Art_ is long, _life_ is brief.
—Seneca)

Jungle Jump!

	Singular	Plural
1st person	-bam	-bāmus
2nd person	-bās	-bātis
3rd person	-bat	-bant

JUNGLE ANTS!

	amō, amāre		videō, vidēre	
PERSON	Singular	Plural	Singular	Plural
1st person	amābam	amābāmus	vidēbam	vidēbāmus
2nd person	amābās	amābātis	vidēbās	vidēbātis
3rd person	amābat	amābant	vidēbat	vidēbant

Spider's Weavings

vocō - I call
arāvī - I plowed
aurī - of gold
bracchium - arm
nāvigō - I sail
vītō - I avoid

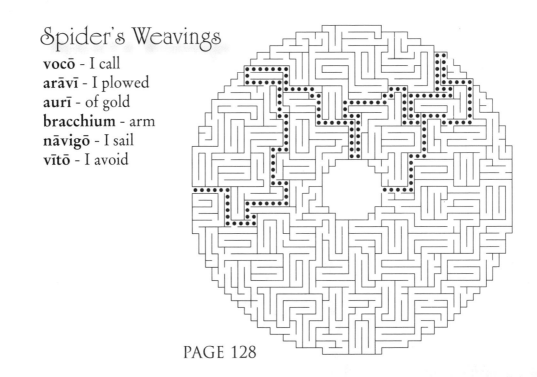

CHAPTER 17

BATTER UP!

```
S S S F R L Y W E H L P J R P
G K I O W K Z U E J V P F F R
B A I L M O N U M E N T Ī U L
S S B I E V Ē L U M M B C L V
Q I U U G N Y X L C I K H W N
O V G M N A T P Ā B U L Ī S A
Y Z I N E E I I M E B J P A T
D C R R Ī U X A U K P S I X U
U G M F C Z P M V M A K J I L
D A Q N N H A W B G F Z H I E
V E R B U M B A R V C F M M F
W P F A T L U F E S K E F M L
D N W P L J L F E I J Q X O V
V Ē L Ī E W U J I H L Z S N A
T O J K H O M X K P U U G U L
Y E F V P C U V K X Y Y S M L
F Q E E E Y U I A A X E L E I
J L W X R R P N L O U Y L N U
S A X U M R B N Q A Q X D I Z
R C Q G P F Ī I H P F R P U F
I H T N E C E L M S N H Q M O
F G S Z N I Q R T Z J V S R L
L C K D V E X S R U M I H J I
D T D S L U M U I U L Q S V I
Z G F C L A K G H G M E H A W
Y V V B C L W K R X N E U L B
P U Y Q Y V V N C E R U Q L W
S U Z W W H C C X D T O M U E
O F H Z O H K D T V S P L M R
J G B O U B S I L E N T I Ī I
```

iron - **ferrum**
of iron - **ferrī**
leaf - **folium**
of leaf - **foliī**
monument - **monumentum**
of monument - **monumentī**
food for animals (fodder) - **pābulum**
of food for animals (fodder) - **pābulī**
rock - **saxum**
of rock - **saxī**
sign - **signum**
of sign - **signī**
silence - **silentium**
of silence - **silentiī**
wall - **vāllum**
of wall - **vallī**
sail - **vēlum**
of sail - **vēlī**
word - **verbum**
of word - **verbī**

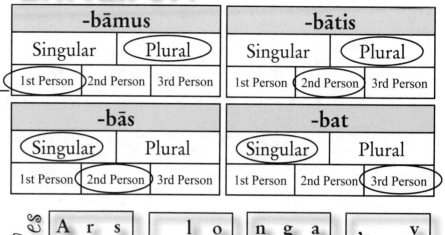

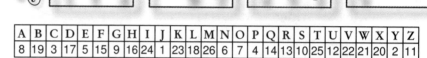

	A	B	C	D	E	F	G	H	I	J	K	L	M	N	O	P	Q	R	S	T	U	V	W	X	Y	Z
	8	19	3	17	5	15	9	16	24	1	23	18	26	6	7	4	14	13	10	25	12	22	21	20	2	11

F E R R U M , I R O N
15 5 13 13 12 26   24 13 7 6

S A X Ī , R O C K (of)
10 8 20   13 7 3 23

F O L I U M , L E A F
15 7 18 24 12 26   18 5 8 15

M O N U M E N T U M , M O N U M E N T
26 7 6 12 26 5 6 25 12 26   26 7 6 12 26 5 6 25

V E R B U M , W O R D
22 5 13 19 12 26   21 7 13 17

V A L L Ī , W A L L
22 8 18 18   21 8 18 18

M O N U M E N T Ī , M O N U M E N T (of)
26 7 6 12 26 5 6 25   26 7 6 12 26 5 6 25

P Ā B U L Ī , F O O D F O R A N I M A L S
4 8 19 12 18   15 7 7 17   15 7 13   8 6 24 26 8 18 10

S A X U M , R O C K
10 8 20 12 26   13 7 3 23

S I L E N T I Ī , S I L E N C E (of)
10 24 18 5 6 25 24   10 24 18 5 6 3 5

S I L E N T I U M , S I L E N C E
10 24 18 5 6 25 24 12 26   10 24 18 5 6 3 5

V Ā L L U M , W A L L
22 8 18 18 12 26   21 8 18 18

P Ā B U L U M , F O O D F O R A N I M A L S
4 8 19 12 18 12 26   15 7 7 17   15 7 13   8 6 24 26 8 18 10

S I G N Ī , S I G N (of)
10 24 9 6   10 24 9 6

V Ē L Ī , S A I L
22 5 18   10 8 24 18

V E R B Ī , W O R D (of)
22 5 13 19   21 7 13 17

F O L I Ī , L E A F
15 7 18 24   18 5 8 15

PAGE 129

CHAPTER 18

videō:	video (movie), vision	
teneō:	tenacious	
habeō:	habitat, habitation (where one lives), habit	
iubeō:	no derivatives	
augeō:	augment, augmentation	
arō:	arable (fit for farming)	
nāvigō:	navigate, navigation, navigator	
vocō:	vocal, vocation	
vītō:	no derivatives (don't confuse with *vita, -ae*, life)	

nauta, -ae:	nautical (relating to seamen, ships, or navigation)
poēta, -ae:	poet, poetry
silentium, -ī:	silent, silence
ager, agri:	agriculture
animus:	animate, animated (spirited, moving)
campus:	camp, campus
folium, -ī:	foliate, foliage
annus:	annual
mūrus:	mural
equus:	equestrian
ferus:	feral (wild), ferocious
verbum, -ī:	verb, verbal, verbose (using a lot of words)

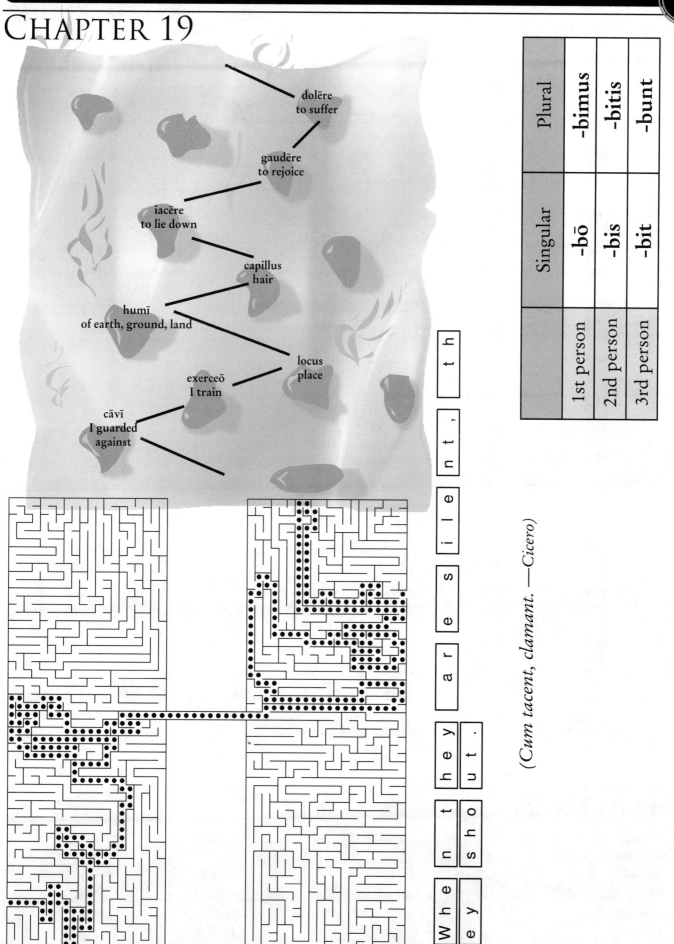

CHAPTER 19

dolēre
to suffer

gaudēre
to rejoice

iacēre
to lie down

capillus
hair

humī
of earth, ground, land

locus
place

exerceō
I train

cāvī
I guarded
against

	Singular		Plural
1st person	-bō		-bimus
2nd person	-bis		-bitis
3rd person	-bit		-bunt

(*Cum tacent, clamant. —Cicero*)

When they are silent, they shout.

CHAPTER 20

	1ST DECLENSION	2ND DECLENSION (M)	2ND DECLENSION (N)
NOM.	-a	-us	-um
GEN.	-ae	-ī	-ī
DAT.	-ae	-ō	-ō
ACC.	-am	-um	-um
ABL.	-ā	-ō	-ō
NOM.	-ae	-ī	-a
GEN.	-ārum	-ōrum	-ōrum
DAT.	-īs	-īs	-īs
ACC.	-ās	-ōs	-a
ABL.	-īs	-īs	-īs

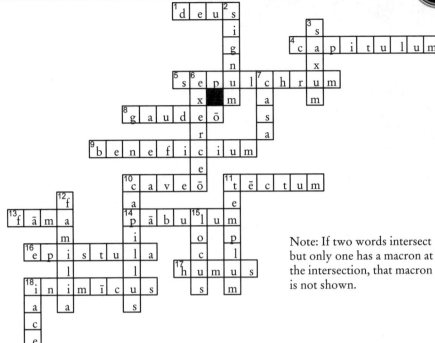

Note: If two words intersect but only one has a macron at the intersection, that macron is not shown.

porta - gate
fossa - ditch
dōnum - gift
īra - anger
serva - female slave
germānus - brother
clāmātum - shouted
dubitāre - to doubt
beneficium - benefit, gift
bonum - good (n)
auxī - I increased
bracchium - arm
iacēre - to lie down
signum - sign
sepulchrum - tomb
ventus - wind
epistula - letter

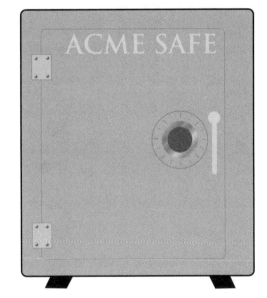

CHAPTER 21

Across
4. I dare
6. to estimate
7. worthy
10. dear
11. long
14. to dare
15. to remain
17. prepared
19. clear
20. I estimated
21. dear
22. clear

Down
1. I grieve
2. I estimate
3. long
5. long
7. worthy
8. worthy
9. I warn
10. dear
12. to warn
13. prepared
15. warned
16. I remain
17. prepared
18. I remained
23. I grieved

Dictum, factum.
(Said and done.
—Terentius)

	Singular	Plural
1st person	eram (*I was*)	erāmus (*we were*)
2nd person	erās (*you were*)	erātis (*you all were*)
3rd person	erat (*he was*)	erant (*they were*)

audeō - I dare
audēre - to dare
ausus sum - I dared
lūgeō - I grieve
lūgēre - to grieve
lūxī - I grieved
lūctum - grieved
moneō - I warn
monēre - to warn
monuī - I warned
monitum - warned
maneō - I remain
manēre - to remain
mānsī - I remained
mānsum - remained
cēnseō - I estimate
cēnsēre - to estimate
cēnsuī - I estimated
cēnsum - estimated
parātus - prepared
parāta - prepared
parātum - prepared
cārus - dear
cāra - dear
cārum - dear
longus - long
longa - long
longum - long
dignus - worthy
digna - worthy
dignum - worthy
clārus - clear
clāra - clearn
clārum - clear

Note: If two words intersect but only one has a macron at the intersection, that macron is not shown.

```
C R M X L B L R K R J V G J Z H C H A A
A Y Z G M B K D S F N C E R V C W U G U
R Q X Q F V W L K I R S F P A R Ā T U S
W S L Q B E E L O N G A U D Ē R E R B U
E X D C N T D I G N U S R C C L Ā R U S
D P O F H Q D K X P G C L Ā R U M T I S
G S M W B I U D I G N U M R T O O G U U
A E N M M R P S G C Ē N S U M A N S U M
B N Y A P P V J V H S S V M O Z E R A O
V L E B M H L M A U V J M A N E Ō Z Z N
E V J V A L L E M E I P C P U I Y E G I
Y P C G W H C G G G M Ā N S Ī L E M L T
H J F S M C I I T B K X C W M A Ū S P U
Y Y M B S U W K J V V J H D L O N G U M
D D Y F W D Q J D M H S G Y S Ū A T E J
X K D X Q L M U N M O H A F A Z X U O Ō
B B O R W D R I C G N M Q W W A P Ī P J
Z R Q O U M X Z V O G P J B S K M M M H
M P R F O X N R L X Z E O A I F L Q C L
E E J C H X C L W L X X V C B L B S B H
C D I G N A A I I A I H C A U T J M T C
A L Ū C T U M R A A B I V J Z Y N J G R
W W Ū H E D O P C M F Z O K S W C P A T
I F I C C E N S E Ō M I E S Q K P U T J
D F M C Ē Ō E J U B E Q U C D T U A S F
C L Ā R Ā R R U Z G W Q M Z H S K B S V
C Ē N S Ē R E J L S J I G R R G E Z R K
H A Ē V P C A U E R S L U M O L L V X M
J Y R Z J Q W I D G N E Q A O F E J V V
M C Ē N S U Ī L X A X N Y E U T S V J W
```

CHAPTER 22

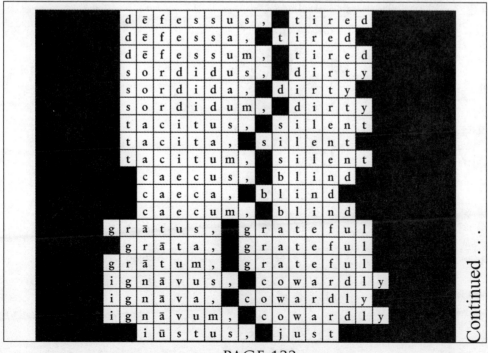

d	ē	f	e	s	s	u	s	,		t	i	r	e	d	
d	ē	f	e	s	s	a	,		t	i	r	e	d		
d	ē	f	e	s	s	u	m	,		t	i	r	e	d	
s	o	r	d	i	d	u	s	,		d	i	r	t	y	
s	o	r	d	i	d	a	,		d	i	r	t	y		
s	o	r	d	i	d	u	m	,		d	i	r	t	y	
t	a	c	i	t	u	s	,		s	i	l	e	n	t	
t	a	c	i	t	a	,		s	i	l	e	n	t		
t	a	c	i	t	u	m	,		s	i	l	e	n	t	

caecus, blind
caeca, blind
caecum, blind
grātus, grateful
grāta, grateful
grātum, grateful
ignāvus, cowardly
ignāva, cowardly
ignāvum, cowardly
iūstus, just

Continued . . . .

... continued

iūsta,	just
iūstum,	just
lātus,	broad
lāta,	broad
lātum,	broad
mīrus,	strange, wonderful
mīra,	strange, wonderful
mīrum,	strange, wonderful
horrendus,	horrendous
horrenda,	horrendous
horrendum,	horrendous

	Present		Imperfect	
	Singular	Plural	Singular	Plural
1st	sum	sumus	eram	erāmus
2nd	es	estis	erās	erātis
3rd	est	sunt	erat	erant

Note: If two words intersect but only one has a macron at the intersection, that macron is not shown.

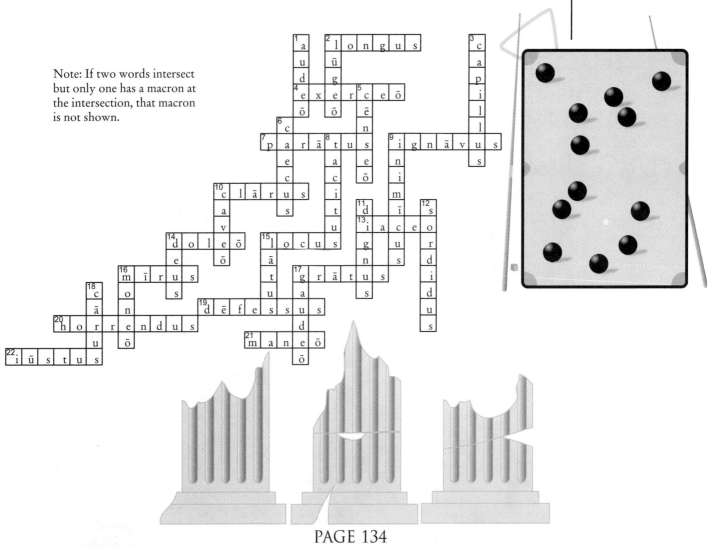

CHAPTER 23

Note: If two words intersect but only one has a macron at the intersection, that macron is not shown.

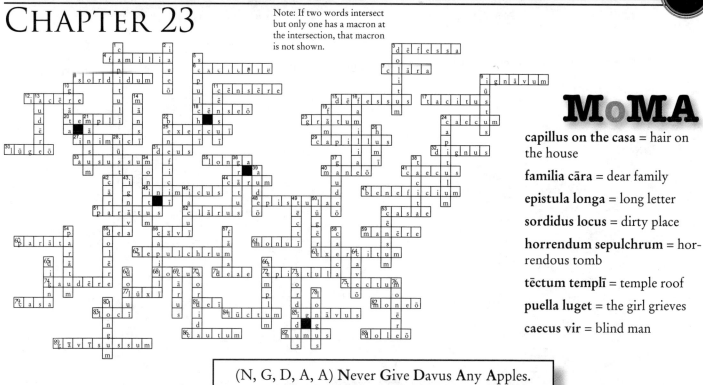

MoMA

capillus on the casa = hair on the house

familia cāra = dear family

epistula longa = long letter

sordidus locus = dirty place

horrendum sepulchrum = horrendous tomb

tēctum templī = temple roof

puella luget = the girl grieves

caecus vir = blind man

(N, G, D, A, A) **N**ever **G**ive **D**avus **A**ny **A**pples.

CHAPTER 24

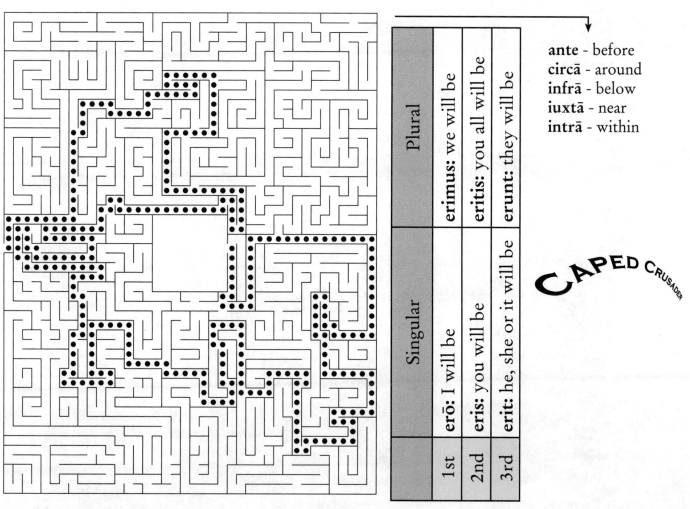

	Plural		
	erimus: we will be	**eritis:** you all will be	**erunt:** they will be
	Singular		
	erō: I will be	**eris:** you will be	**erit:** he, she or it will be
	1st	2nd	3rd

ante - before
circā - around
infrā - below
iuxtā - near
intrā - within

CAPED CRUSADER

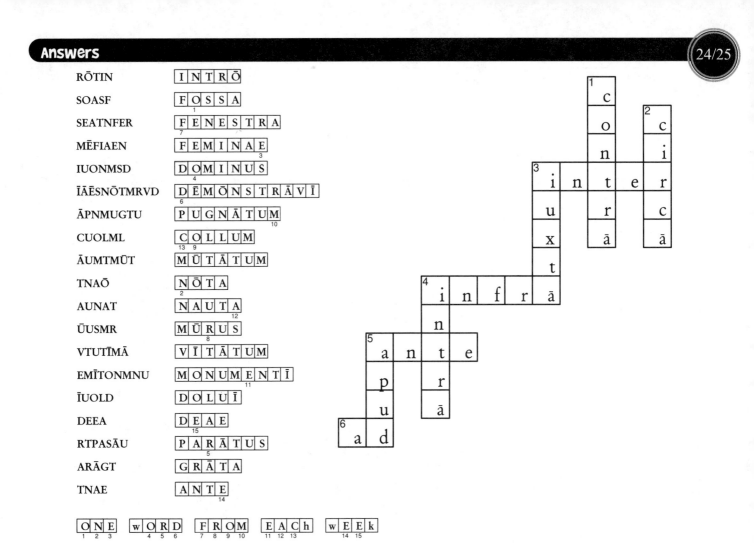

RŌTIN	I N T R Ō
SOASF	F O S S A
SEATNFER	F E N E S T R A
MĒFIAEN	F E M I N A E
IUONMSD	D O M I N U S
ĪĀĒSNŌTMRVD	D Ē M Ō N S T R Ā V Ī
ĀPNMUGTU	P U G N Ā T U M
CUOLML	C O L L U M
ĀUMTMŪT	M Ū T Ā T U M
TNAŌ	N Ō T A
AUNAT	N A U T A
ŪUSMR	M Ū R U S
VTUTĪMĀ	V Ī T Ā T U M
EMĪTONMNU	M O N U M E N T Ī
ĪUOLD	D O L U Ī
DEEA	D E A E
RTPASĀU	P A R Ā T U S
ARĀGT	G R Ā T A
TNAE	A N T E

O N E   w O R D   F R O M   E A C h   w E E k

CHAPTER 25

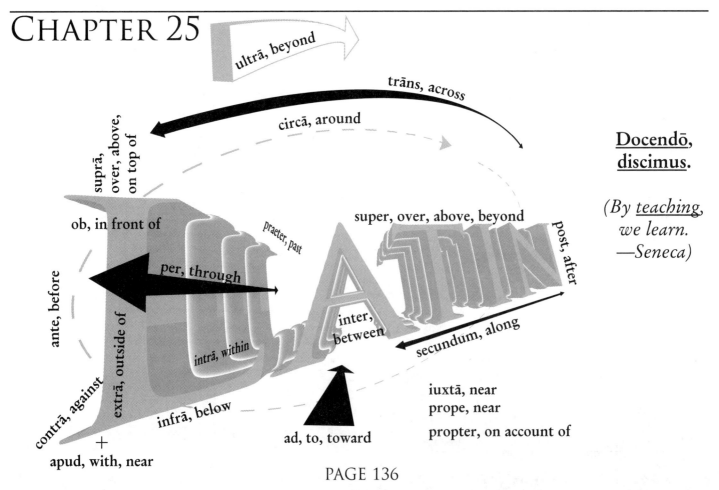

ultrā, beyond

trāns, across

circā, around

suprā, over, above, on top of

super, over, above, beyond

ob, in front of

praeter, past

post, after

ante, before

per, through

inter, between

secundum, along

extrā, outside of

intrā, within

contrā, against

infrā, below

ad, to, toward

iuxtā, near
prope, near
propter, on account of

+

apud, with, near

Docendō, discimus.

(By teaching, we learn. —Seneca)

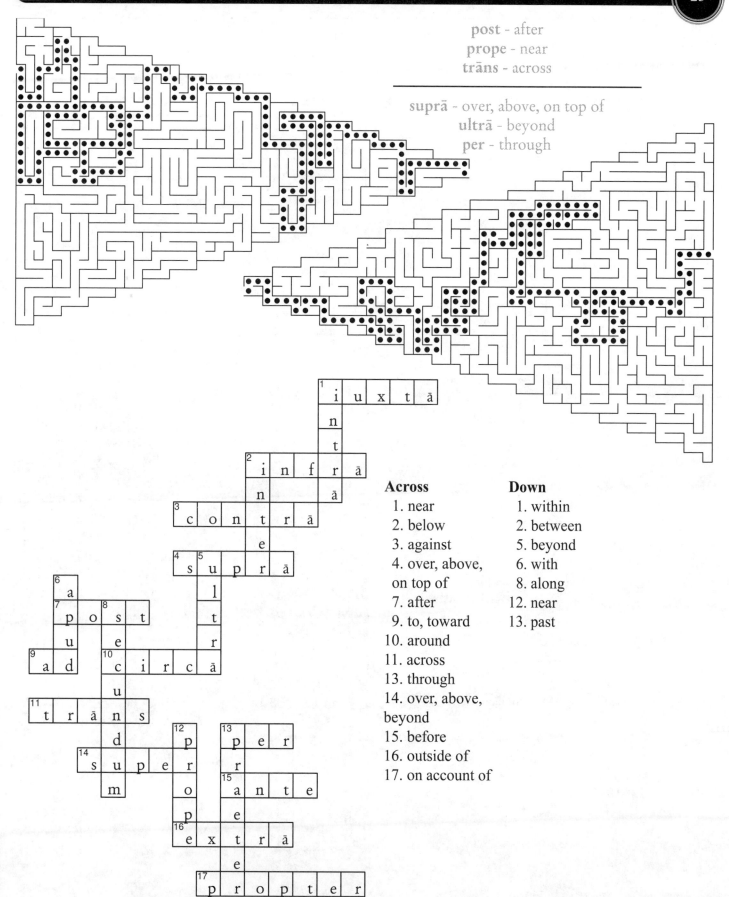

post - after
prope - near
trāns - across

suprā - over, above, on top of
ultrā - beyond
per - through

Across
1. near
2. below
3. against
4. over, above, on top of
7. after
9. to, toward
10. around
11. across
13. through
14. over, above, beyond
15. before
16. outside of
17. on account of

Down
1. within
2. between
5. beyond
6. with
8. along
12. near
13. past

CHAPTER 26

	Singular	Plural
1st person	sum *I am*	sumus *we are*
2nd person	es *you are*	estis *you all are*
3rd person	est *he is*	sunt *they are*

	Singular	Plural
1st person	eram *I was*	erāmus *we were*
2nd person	erās *you were*	erātis *you all were*
3rd person	erat *he was*	erant *they were*

	Singular	Plural
1st person	erō *I will be*	erimus *we will be*
2nd person	eris *you will be*	eritis *you all will be*
3rd person	erit *he will be*	erunt *they will be*

The Big Race!

74, ad	add, address
08, ante	antebellum, antecedent, anteroom
88, apud	no derivatives
66, circā	circus, circle, circulate
61, contrā	contrary, contradict
19, extrā	extraordinary, extraterrestrial
21, infrā	infrared, infrastructure
39, inter	interest, intersperse, interact
51, intrā	introvert, intravenous
12, iuxtā	juxtapose, juxtaposition
48, ob	observe, oblong, obsess
66, per	perfect, per chance, perennial
04, praeter	preternatural
93, prope	propinquity
91, secundum	second, secondary
38, super	supersonic, supercharge, supercomputer
56, suprā	supranational
18, trāns	transfer, transform, transact

```
A F T E R M A K B I U J P I J F B C R N
R O X D B C Q H V E I N Z X D J E I A A
I M K T O D Z L K C Y P C O X F R W P
O N B E T W E E N P R O P T E R O C I U
S W T U Y N S X W I T I N T E R R A T D
Y U D R Z W O E T U A H E D H A E O H P
R S P A A V V M C U L T R A O Z P U I O
A G G R O B E F I U O A R O U N D T N S
Q N G U A N R J O Q N O R X U B B S V T
N V I R L J A H B D G C X C G T I G T
Y E F E T B B C W D E S U Q D Q H D G N
B Z A U R D O G C F G N W M D K K E J H
E X T R A B V M N O I N F R O N T O F P
L B G N N T E S O Z U L E P I V O F M R
O K Q F S K O A W X X N Q A U K P R L A
W R O K Y A N C X D T D T X R P G X D E
N U R K K T T L O K A S D O J Z O X G T
Z Q Q O R H O L K N W I P H F H D B H E
L N R Q P E P W I F T A I C V P A S T R
O W F M X E O H A N Z R C P I L O T T K
A G S L J C F S W R F F A E R U G E O K
A W I T H F E B L X D R J R I M C T L R
G O S P D M H B J F Y U A L J L S Q A D
A D F F J H K T F H B I K O F U O O Q F
I Q P B S C L Y Y V B W J B J M U A G N
N A C R O S S U P E R W R A F C E B X U
S X X N P S W V M Y P H T J X H X K D W
T Q H O L O A K E S P O G O E K C E Z I
F G X R F H V W X U Z Q B B A L M U J B
O V E R A B O V E B E Y O N D T T E A D
```

CHAPTER 27

	Singular	Plural
1st person	eō (*I go*)	īmus (*we go*)
2nd person	īs (*you go*)	ītis (*you all go*)
3rd person	it (*he goes*)	eunt (*they go*)

GŌRO — R O G Ō (12)

XIIEMTERSĀ — E X I S T I M Ā R E (13)

OĪGRVĀ — R O G Ā V Ī (10)

SMSIEAP — P E S S I M A (2)

TĀPROE — O P T Ā R E (3)

TTMPOĀU — O P T Ā T U M

MISVXĀĪETI — E X I S T I M Ā V Ī (4)

MDNŪU — N Ū D U M

RUŪDS — D Ū R U S (9)

ĀTĪOPV — O P T Ā V Ī (16)

DVĪĀŌN — D Ō N Ā V Ī

ŌE — E Ō

OĀGRER — R O G Ā R E (15)

TGUĀRMO — R O G Ā T U M

MAIMIN — M I N I M A (6)

ASLTU — A L T U S (1)

LAUMT — A L T U M (14)

UTŌNĀMD — D Ō N Ā T U M (5)

ŌDĀERN — D Ō N Ā R E (7)

IMMMUIN — M I N I M U M (8)

MSISMEUP — P E S S I M U M (11)

L A T I N   w A R M S   y O U R   h E A R T !
1 2 3 4 5   6 7 8 9   10 11 12   13 14 15 16

CHAPTER 28

rēcta - straight
proxima - near
ultima - farthest
plēnum - full
reliquum - remaining

pūrus - pure
varia - various
rēctum - straight
plēnus - full
reliqua - remaining

ultimus - farthest
rēctum - straight

TERRA

LATIN BINGO!

		Plural	Singular
Imperfect	Plural	ībāmus, ībātis, ībant	
	Singular		ībam, ībās, ībat
Future	Plural	ībimus, ībitis, ībunt	
	Singular		ībō, ībis, ībit
Present	Plural	īmus, ītis, eunt	
	Singular		eō, īs, it
			1st, 2nd, 3rd

CHAPTER 29

cum - with
sine - without
prae - in front of
ex - out of

A	B	C	D	E	F	G	H	I	J	K	L	M	N	O	P	Q	R	S	T	U	V	W	X	Y	Z
1	23	5	9	14	20	11	2	25	16	19	8	21	15	13	10	18	26	3	22	6	24	12	7	4	17

Ā OR AB, FROM, BY
13 26 / 1 23 / 20 26 13 21 / 23 4

CORAM, FACE-TO-FACE
5 13 26 1 21 / 20 1 5 14 / 22 13 / 20 1 5 14

WITH
12 25 22 2

CUM, WITH
5 6 21 / 12 25 22 2

DĒ, DOWN FROM, FROM
9 / 9 13 12 15 / 20 26 13 21 / 20 26 13 21

Ē OR EX, OUT OF
13 26 / 14 7 / 13 6 22 / 13 20

IN + ABLATIVE, IN
25 15 / 1 23 8 1 22 25 24 14 / 25 15

IN + ACCUSATIVE, INTO
25 15 / 1 5 5 6 3 1 22 25 24 14 / 25 15 22 13

PRAE, IN FRONT OF
10 26 1 14 / 25 15 / 20 26 13 15 22 / 13 20

PRŌ, BEFORE, ON BEHALF
10 26 / 23 14 20 13 26 14 / 13 15 / 23 14 2 1 8 20

OF
13 20

SINE, WITHOUT
3 25 15 14 / 12 25 22 2 13 6 22

SUB + ABLATIVE, UNDER
3 6 23 / 1 23 8 1 22 25 24 14 / 6 15 9 14 26

SUB + ACCUSATIVE, UP
3 6 23 / 1 5 5 6 3 1 22 25 24 14 / 6 10

TO
22 13

TENUS, TO THE EXTENT
22 14 15 6 3 / 22 13 / 22 2 14 / 14 7 22 14 15 22

OF, UP TO, DOWN TO, AS
13 20 / 6 10 / 22 13 / 9 13 12 15 / 22 13 / 1 3

FAR AS
20 1 26 / 1 3

ā or ab - from, by
cōram - face-to-face with
cum - with
dē - down from, from
ē or ex - out of
in + ablative - in
in + accusative - into
prae - in front of
prō - before, on behalf of
sine - without
sub + ablative - under
sub + accusative - up to
tenus - to the extent of, up to, down to, as far as

CHAPTER 30

Note: If two words intersect but only one has a macron at the intersection, that macron is not shown.

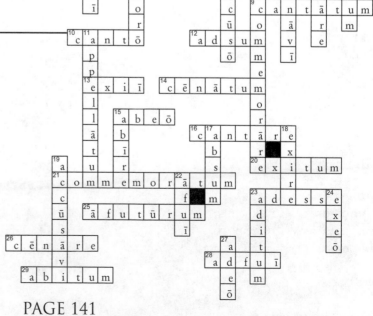

	Present		Imperfect		Future	
	Singular	Plural	Singular	Plural	Singular	Plural
1st	sum	sumus	eram	erāmus	erō	erimus
2nd	es	estis	erās	erātis	eris	eritis
3rd	est	sunt	erat	erant	eris	erunt

absum - I am absent
abesse - to be absent
āfuī - I was absent
āfutūrum - absent
adsum - I am present
adesse - to be present
adfuī - I was present
adfutūrum - present
abeō - I go away
abīre - to go away
abiī - I went away
abitum - gone
adeō - I approach
adīre - to approach
adiī - I approached
aditum - approached
exeō - I go out
exīre - to go out
exiī - I went out
exitum - gone out
cēnō - I dine
cēnāre - to dine
cēnāvī - I dined
cēnātum - dined
cantō - I sing
cantāre - to sing
cantāvī - I sang
cantātum - sung
appellō - I name
appellāre - to name
appellāvī - I named
appellātum - named
accūsō - I accuse
accūsāre - to accuse
accūsāvī - I accused
accūsātum - accused
commemorō - I remember
commemorāre - to remember
commemorāvī - I remembered
commemorātum - remembered

```
C Q W Z P P Y C T Z K Z D T A
S O Q U I U G U X M F Z R J P
C O M M E M O R Ā T U M Z L P
A V K M A P P E L L Ā T U M E
D B T U F G Q X G S M V E L
Ī R Ī L L M Z Q A E A Y C S L
R X Q R Z C O D I K Ō Z S G Ā
E Z F I E W Ē R A B E Ō U D R
U B Y Y X G W N Ā V J O C V E
M B G R L J H C Ā R Y N L C S
A T C D V N L O I R E U J F S
A F U T Ū R U M A D E S S E Z
E R Z V J L C M M B V Y M T Y
X G P C A P P E L L Ā V Ī A Ā
Ī U H E A D M M N F C U Q B F
Ī Q A H L N A O R Ā J U R E U
N R O B K L T R M A T S D S Ī
A C C Ū S Ō Ō Ā E D X U J S J
Z C Ē N Ō U D V T S X C M E C
L W C L I E M Ī Y U S A H L O
B V B Ū A D F U Ī M M N C A M
H Q B W S D G G O L E T A C M
U D A D J Ā P S V A K Ā A C E
I I E D L V T B H E L R D Ū M
C W E C F I O U G R O E Ī S O
Ē H E S G U W R M W F H T Ā R
N Q F C A N T Ā V Ī L W U R Ō
Ā L P F A C C Ū S Ā V Ī M E A
V E X Ī R E A A R A D Ī Ī C D
Ī L Q E A H Y N B U H X A D E
T O D O H B W X T Ī M P P F Ō
I G I G T J L U O Ō Ī Z W C L
D I H J E H P T D Q K F S S Z
K R R T I K F F U E X I T U M
U Q W L Z X Y X Q M Y Y V M S
```

Note: If two words intersect but only one has a macron at the intersection, that macron is not shown.

PAGE 142

CHAPTER 31

ACROSS

2. I go
4. I choose
6. pure (n)
7. I dine
8. to ask
9. to accuse
10. I sing
12. various (m)
17. to sing
19. I went out
20. to go
21. high
23. dined
24. smallest (m)
26. near (n)
28. farthest (n)
30. gone
33. high (m)
34. to give
35. gone
36. I judge
38. smallest (f)
39. worst (f)
40. I was absent
41. I am absent
42. I went away

DOWN

1. I named
2. judged
3. I give
5. pure (m)
7. face-to-face with
9. named
11. to go away
13. present
14. in
15. high (f)
16. worst (n)
18. I approach
22. down from, concerning, about
25. chosen
27. straight (n)
28. farthest (m)
29. smallest (n)
30. I accuse
31. worst (m)
32. I gave
36. I go out
37. with

varius	various, variety, variable
dūrus	durable, endure
ultimus	ultimate, ultimately, ultimatum
plēnus	plenty, plenary
pūrus	pure, purify
rogō	interrogate, interrogatory
rēctus	rectify, rectangle, rectitude
prō	produce, proceed, progress
ā or ab	abnormal, abduct, abort
ē or ex	exhale, exclude, expect
altus	altitude, altimeter, alps
in + ablative	inhale, include, inspect, import
sub + ablative	submarine, submerge, subplot
absum	absent, absentee
minimus	minimal, minimum, mini
exeō	exit
optō	opt, option, optional
accūsō	accuse, accusation, accusatory
commemorō	commemorate, commemorative, commemoration

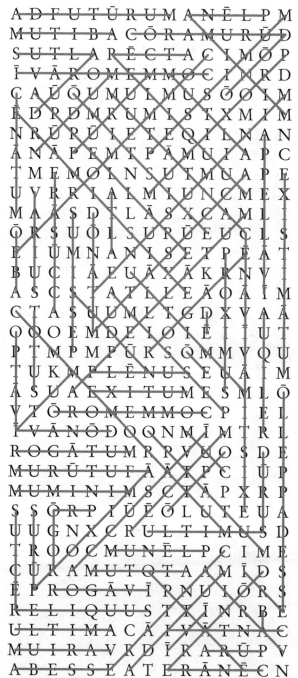

CHAPTER 32

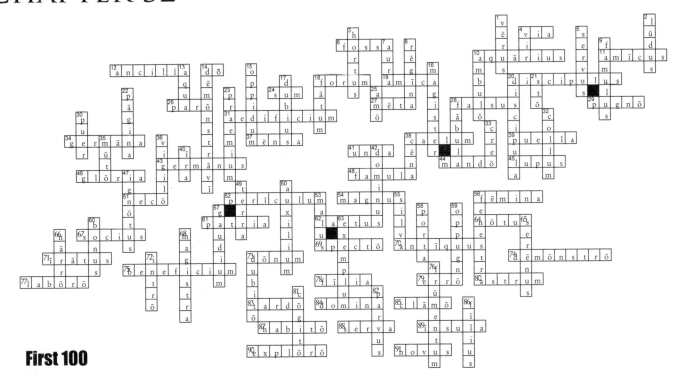

First 100

Note: If two words intersect but only
one has a macron at the intersection, that
macron is not shown.

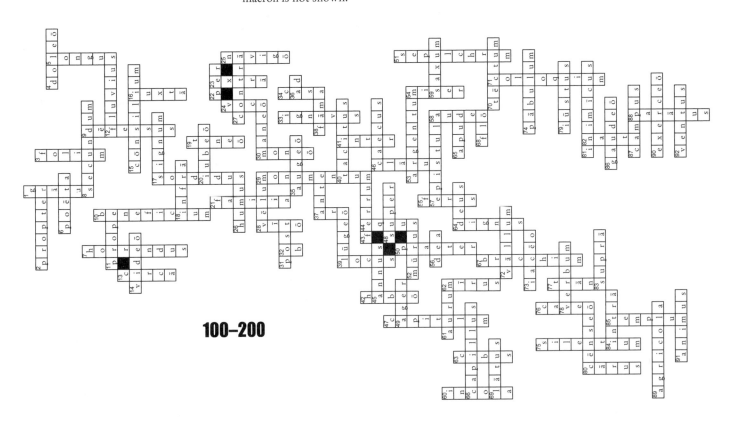

100–200

K L C W L
Z S S O N
~~D E~~ ī J D
Y B O F P
Q E I O A

Note: If two words intersect but only one has a macron at the intersection, that macron is not shown.

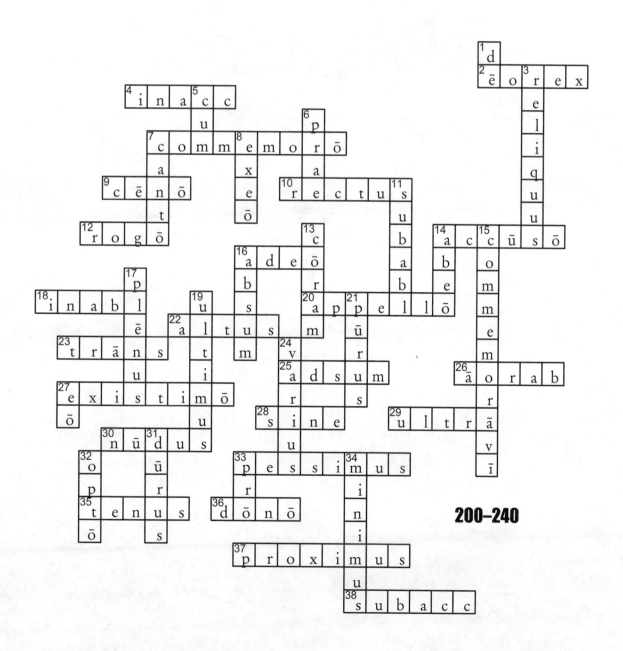

200–240

LATIN
on the
High Seas!™

GROUP GAME
BASED ON *LATIN FOR CHILDREN PRIMER A*

Latin on the High Seas!™ is a game intended for group play between 2 to 10 players (or even a whole classroom).

Backstory:

Journal Entry: Argh, 63 days out at sea and no land in bloomin' sight. Our food stores have either dwindled to little more than crumbs or gone rancid o'er a week ago. Even the rancid pork was scarfed down yesterday, yet not without its revenge. We need to find land soon so that our boys can find food and water. Oh, if the Good Lord above would just grant us a northeaster so as to catch us some good rain water, or the eyes to spot a coconut or two adrift on the water to eat . . .

Rules:

Each "seaman" (player) receives a ***Latin on the High Seas!***™ playing card (1 of 12). The "captain" (leader, parent, or teacher) then slowly reads English words, randomly chosen, off the included "cargo" list (English translations), giving the seamen an appropriate amount of time to translate the item into Latin. The captain should check off each item presented from the cargo list for record. Each seaman, having quietly translated the item into Latin, then quickly searches for that Latin word on his or her card. If that Latin word is found on the card, the seaman will place a coin (pennies, nickels, buttons, etc.) over the Latin word. If the Latin word is not on the card, the seaman will await the next item from the cargo list. Play continues until the first person reaches 10 points.

Point System:

To gain points in ***Latin on the High Seas!***™ a seaman must have on his or her player card a sequence of coins (covered Latin words) that matches at least one of the patterns below:

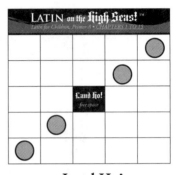

Coconuts!	**Rainstorm!**	**Land Ho!**
Food found in the water.	**Water gathered.**	**Land spotted.**
Worth = 1 point	Worth = 2 points	Worth = 3 points

At least 2 coins need to be mirroring themselves across from the "Land Ho! Free Space" square. They can be horizontal, vertical, or diagonal. Pairs must touch the free space.

Coins must occupy all four corners.

Must have 5 coins in a row. The coins can incorporate the free space. They can be vertical, horizontal, or diagonal. Coins must be in a straight row or column.

A seaman must verbally claim points by crying aloud "Coconuts!" "Rainstorm!" or "Land ho!" when such patterns have been found on the playing card. When "Coconuts" or "Rainstorm" is called out, the captain reviews the pattern (for correct placement), records the score, and game play continues. When "Land ho!" is cried out, the captain reviews the pattern (for correct placement), records the score, and has all of the seamen remove their coins from their playing cards to begin the game afresh (unless 10 points have been tallied by one individual).

Water, water, everywhere . . .

If multiple cries arise at the same time, all of the patterns are reviewed, and all seamen with completed patterns receive points. There is no limit to how many "Coconuts" and "Rainstorms" can be claimed by seamen within the same game.

Points for "Land ho!" are only given to the first player to accurately cry it aloud. No other points, regardless of patterns, are recorded for that game upon the correct cry of "Land ho!"

Player Cards:

Note: There are <u>two different sets</u> of player cards and cargo lists. The first set is labeled for use with *Latin for Children Primer A* chapters 1 to 15. The second set is for use with *Latin for Children Primer A* chapters 1 to 30.

Enjoy, maties!
And may the wind be at your back!

Alternate Rules:
- For a longer or shorter game, fluctuate the ending point goal by either raising or lowering it.
- Add additional patterns with their own point scheme to the game for extra fun.

Note for Captains:

You may want to photocopy a dozen copies of the cargo list before playing. That way, with each game you play, you can have students use a fresh list, making it easier to review a seaman's player card when points are found.

Or, use colored pens (one color per game) to check off words from the cargo list to help delineate the markings of each game.

Chapters 1–15

LATIN on the High Seas! ™
Latin for Children Primer A • CHAPTERS 1–15

tardō	hortus	habitō	frūmentum	pāgina
aquārius	puella	oppidum	amō	auxilium
intrō	oppugnāre	**Land Ho!** *free space*	praemium	mēnsa
beneficium	aura	parō	pugnō	hortus
dō	mandō	dēmōnstrō	gaudium	fossa

LATIN on the High Seas! ™
Latin for Children Primer A • CHAPTERS 1–15

amīca	fenestra	tardō	fātum	dēmōnstrō
stō	aqua	puella	labōrō	pugnō
perīculum	hortus	**Land Ho!** *free space*	frūmentum	fēmina
amō	collum	sum	patria	porta
cēna	hortus	lūdus	nārrō	habitō

LATIN on the High Seas!™
Latin for Children, Primer A • CHAPTERS 1–15

puer	oppidum	lupus	terra	glōria
perīculum	fābula	spectō	aquārius	praemium
dēmōnstrō	ambulō	**Land Ho!** *free space*	astrum	intrō
fenestra	tardō	mēta	beneficium	collum
silva	gaudium	necō	cēna	mandō

LATIN on the High Seas!™
Latin for Children Primer A • CHAPTERS 1–15

glōria	fīlia	puer	caelum	amō
puella	aedificium	fēmina	necō	dōnum
auxilium	discipula	**Land Ho!** *free space*	sum	tardō
amīca	nārrō	fātum	perīculum	oppidum
gaudium	ambulō	frūmentum	beneficium	fossa

Chapters 1–15

labōrō	stō	lūdus	fenestra	via
forum	aedificium	habitō	germānus	magistra
collum	amīcus	**Land Ho!** *free space*	dō	praemium
fīlius	aqua	mandō	astrum	parō
frūmentum	fēmina	pātria	hortus	ambulō

unda	praemium	fēmina	amīca	porta
puellae	vigilō	caelum	fīlia	magistra
oppidum	aquārius	**Land Ho!** *free space*	oppugnāre	cēna
discipulus	gaudium	intrō	forum	fenestra
beneficium	pāgina	auxilium	īnsula	aedificium

LATIN on the High Seas! ™
Latin for Children Primer A • CHAPTERS 1–15

fīlia	lupus	serva	terra	hortus
necō	fīlius	magister	pugnō	unda
famulus	exemplum	**Land Ho!** *free space*	nārrō	perīculum
puellae	fābula	amīcus	praemium	germānus
fenestra	frūmentum	discipulus	īnsula	collum

LATIN on the High Seas! ™
Latin for Children Primer A • CHAPTERS 1–15

lupus	caelum	serva	amō	vigilō
exemplum	silva	necō	dōnum	aura
īra	pugnō	**Land Ho!** *free space*	pātria	auxilium
vir	discipula	astrum	ancilla	amīca
puella	dominus	labōrō	perīculum	errō

Chapters 1–15

LATIN on the High Seas! ™
Latin for Children Primer A • CHAPTERS 1–15

forum	oppugnāre	amīcus	intrō	puer
mēta	gaudium	germāna	discipulus	vir
famulus	socius	**Land Ho!** *free space*	puella	īra
dō	beneficium	rēgīna	collum	oppidum
spectō	famula	exemplum	lupus	porta

LATIN on the High Seas! ™
Latin for Children Primer A • CHAPTERS 1–15

servus	forum	germāna	discipulus	glōria
amīca	dominus	nārrō	caelum	socius
discipula	astrum	**Land Ho!** *free space*	fēmina	ancilla
oppidum	unda	gaudium	spectō	famula
via	hortus	domina	pātria	mēnsa

Chapters 1–15

LATIN on the High Seas! ™
Latin for Children Primer A • CHAPTERS 1–15

fossa	clāmō	fīlia	unda	dōnum
astrum	mandō	collum	famulus	lupus
puella	glōria	**Land Ho!** *free space*	fābula	aquārius
fātum	beneficium	exemplum	discipula	spectō
puer	habitō	lūdus	frūmentum	magister

LATIN on the High Seas! ™
Latin for Children Primer A • CHAPTERS 1–15

unda	nārrō	lupus	discipula	errō
labōrō	astrum	oppugnāre	dōnum	domina
servus	clāmō	**Land Ho!** *free space*	socius	glōria
puer	collum	fīlia	gaudium	rēgīna
magister	mandō	amīcus	amō	lūdus

CARGO LIST 1

- amō - I love
- dō - I give
- intrō - I enter
- labōrō - I work
- nārrō - I tell
- aqua - water
- fābula - story
- porta - gate
- silva - forest
- terra - earth
- via - road, way
- fossa - ditch
- mēnsa - table
- mēta - turning point, goal
- pāgina - page
- cēna - dinner
- patria - fatherland, country
- aura - breeze
- rēgīna - queen
- īnsula - island
- errō - I wander
- stō - I stand
- parō - I prepare
- spectō - I look at
- sum - I am
- ancilla - maidservant
- glōria - glory
- īra - anger
- unda - wave
- fenestra - window
- puella - girl
- fēmina - woman
- fīlia - daughter
- germāna - sister
- magistra - teacher (female)
- discipula - student (female)
- domina - master (female)
- famula - servant (female)
- serva - slave (female)
- amīca - friend (female)
- puellae - girl

- puer - boy
- vir - man
- germānus - brother
- fīlius - son
- magister - teacher/master (male)
- discipulus - student/disciple (male)
- dominus - master (male)
- famulus - servant (male)
- servus - slave (male)
- amīcus - friend (male)
- vigilō - I watch (or guard)
- clāmō - I shout
- tardō - I delay
- habitō - I live
- dēmōnstrō - I point out
- lūdus - school, game, play
- hortus - garden
- lupus - wolf
- socius - ally, associate
- aquārius - water-carrier
- pugnō - I fight
- oppugnāre - to attack
- necō - I kill
- ambulō - I walk
- mandō - I entrust
- aedificium - building
- caelum - sky
- auxilium - help
- exemplum - example
- dōnum - gift
- fātum - fate
- forum - public square
- oppidum - town
- perīculum - danger
- frūmentum - grain
- praemium - reward
- astrum - star
- beneficium - benefit, gift
- gaudium - joy
- collum - neck

CARGO LIST 2

Latin for Children Primer A • <u>CHAPTERS 1–30</u>

- ☐ amō - I love
- ☐ aqua - water
- ☐ silva - forest
- ☐ terra - earth
- ☐ aura - breeze
- ☐ īnsula - island
- ☐ glōria - glory
- ☐ puella - girl
- ☐ fēmina - woman
- ☐ fīlia - daughter
- ☐ amīca - friend (female)
- ☐ puellae - girl
- ☐ puer - boy
- ☐ vir - man
- ☐ germānus - brother
- ☐ auxilium - help
- ☐ astrum - star
- ☐ beneficium - benefit, gift
- ☐ gaudium - joy
- ☐ nāvigō - I sail
- ☐ flō - I blow
- ☐ vocō - I call
- ☐ vītō - I avoid
- ☐ aurum - gold
- ☐ argentum - silver
- ☐ colloquium - conversation
- ☐ cōnsilium - plan
- ☐ folium - leaf
- ☐ saxum - rock
- ☐ signum - sign
- ☐ silentium - silence
- ☐ vēlum - sail
- ☐ verbum - word
- ☐ caveō - I guard against
- ☐ exerceō - I train
- ☐ gaudeō - I rejoice
- ☐ iaceō - I lie down
- ☐ deus - god
- ☐ capillus - hair
- ☐ casa - house

- ☐ epistula - letter
- ☐ fāma - fame
- ☐ familia - family
- ☐ sepulchrum - tomb
- ☐ tēctum - roof
- ☐ templum - temple
- ☐ lūgeō - I grieve
- ☐ moneō - I warn
- ☐ maneō - I remain
- ☐ cēnseō - I estimate
- ☐ parātus - prepared
- ☐ cārus - dear
- ☐ longus - long
- ☐ dignus - worthy
- ☐ clārus - clear
- ☐ dēfessus - tired
- ☐ sordidus - dirty
- ☐ grātus - grateful
- ☐ iūstus - just
- ☐ lātus - broad
- ☐ horrendus - horrendous
- ☐ ad - to, toward
- ☐ ante - before
- ☐ apud - at, by, near
- ☐ circā - around
- ☐ contrā - against
- ☐ extrā - outside of
- ☐ inter - between, among
- ☐ intrā - within
- ☐ iuxtā - near, next to
- ☐ per - through
- ☐ post - after
- ☐ praeter - past
- ☐ prope - near
- ☐ secundum - along
- ☐ trāns - across
- ☐ ultrā - beyond
- ☐ optō - I choose
- ☐ existimō - I judge
- ☐ dōnō - I give
- ☐ eō - I go

- ☐ īvī - I went
- ☐ itum - gone
- ☐ dūrus - hard
- ☐ minimus - smallest
- ☐ pessimus - worst
- ☐ pūrus - pure
- ☐ rēctus - straight
- ☐ reliquus - remaining
- ☐ proximus - nearest
- ☐ ultimus - farthest
- ☐ varius - various
- ☐ ā or ab - from, by
- ☐ cōram - face-to-face with
- ☐ cum - with
- ☐ dē - down from, from
- ☐ ē or ex - out of
- ☐ in + ablative - in
- ☐ in + accusative - into
- ☐ prae - in front of
- ☐ prō - before, on behalf of
- ☐ sine - without
- ☐ sub + ablative - under
- ☐ sub + accusative - up to
- ☐ adsum - I am present
- ☐ adeō - I approach
- ☐ exeō - I go out
- ☐ cantō - I sing
- ☐ accūsō - I accuse

Chapters 1–30

LATIN on the High Seas! ™
Latin for Children Primer A • Chapters 1–30

inter	reliquus	fīlia	prae	epistula
sub + accusative	optō	cum	contrā	adsum
deus	minimus	**Land Ho!** *free space*	varius	grātus
vocō	sub + ablative	ad	capillus	itum
silentium	horrendus	dignus	proximus	pūrus

LATIN on the High Seas! ™
Latin for Children Primer A • Chapters 1–30

adeō	cantō	lātus	deus	dignus
iaceō	per	existimō	grātus	exeō
proximus	varius	**Land Ho!** *free space*	prae	īnsula
dēfessus	ultrā	eō	ē or ex	minimus
contrā	cum	itum	vocō	optō

LATIN on the High Seas!™
Latin for Children Primer A • Chapters 1–30

intrā	pessimus	maneō	in + accusative	silva
dōnō	silentium	sub + ablative	ante	ā or ab
pūrus	eō	**Land Ho!** *free space*	dē	horrendus
nāvigō	capillus	adsum	vītō	cum
exeō	ad	extrā	per	glōria

LATIN on the High Seas!™
Latin for Children Primer A • Chapters 1–30

prope	fēmina	in + ablative	reliquus	ad
itum	familia	ē or ex	intrā	saxum
dēfessus	optō	**Land Ho!** *free space*	lātus	proximus
casa	epistula	dōnō	ultrā	moneō
prae	silva	varius	vītō	cōram

LATIN on the High Seas!™
Latin for Children, Primer A • Chapters 1–30

sine	īvī	casa	pessimus	extrā
terra	post	dē	existimō	amō
ā or ab	fāma	**Land Ho!** *free space*	sordidus	dūrus
maneō	praeter	beneficium	nāvigō	templum
ultimus	exerceō	apud	ante	silentium

LATIN on the High Seas!™
Latin for Children Primer A • Chapters 1–30

amīca	ad	sub + accusative	reliquus	eō
aurum	minimus	pūrus	sordidus	sub + ablative
cōram	lūgeō	**Land Ho!** *free space*	adsum	flō
inter	moneō	verbum	post	familia
īvī	sepulchrum	templum	trāns	puellae

Chapters 1–30

LATIN on the High Seas! ™
Latin for Children Primer A • Chapters 1–30

folium	in + accusative	prope	germānus	ē or ex
apud	aurum	argentum	praeter	grātus
clārus	ā or ab	**Land Ho!** *free space*	iūstus	parātus
trāns	vēlum	flō	gaudium	fāma
ultrā	aqua	dūrus	lūgeō	proximus

LATIN on the High Seas! ™
Latin for Children Primer A • Chapters 1–30

accūsō	in + ablative	dignus	in + accusative	adeō
auxilium	clārus	adsum	argentum	prope
caveō	īvī	**Land Ho!** *free space*	sine	ultimus
dē	cārus	existimō	terra	praeter
saxum	grātus	proximus	vēlum	ad

LATIN on the High Seas!™
Latin for Children Primer A • Chapters 1–30

prō	reliquus	rēctus	aqua	caveō
cōnsilium	dēfessus	dignus	trāns	clārus
proximus	cēnseō	**Land Ho!** *free space*	folium	ā or ab
dūrus	secundum	adeō	cārus	iuxtā
iūstus	puella	sepulchrum	pūrus	gaudeō

LATIN on the High Seas!™
Latin for Children Primer A • Chapters 1–30

sub + accusative	trāns	circā	exerceō	ultimus
cōram	iaceō	signum	dēfessus	in + accusative
aura	varius	**Land Ho!** *free space*	reliquus	astrum
iuxtā	verbum	dōnō	pessimus	cōnsilium
auxilium	argentum	existimō	prō	cēnseō